THE COLD WAR, 1945–1991

Studies in European History

Series Editors: John Breuilly
Julian Jackson
Peter Wilson

The Cold War, 1945–1991

Second edition

Michael L. Dockrill and Michael F. Hopkins

First edition published 1988
Second edition published 2006 by
PALGRAVE MACMILLAN
Houndmills, Basingstoke, Hampshire RG21 6XS and
175 Fifth Avenue, New York, N.Y. 10010
Companies and representatives throughout the world

PALGRAVE MACMILLAN is the global academic imprint of the Palgrave
Macmillan division of St. Martin's Press, LLC and of Palgrave Macmillan Ltd.
Macmillan® is a registered trademark in the United States, United Kingdom
and other countries. Palgrave is a registered trademark in the European
Union and other countries.

ISBN-13: 978-1-4039-3338-6 paperback
ISBN-10: 1-4039-3338-3 paperback

This book is printed on paper suitable for recycling and made from fully
managed and sustained forest sources.

A catalogue record for this book is available from the British Library.

A catalog record for this book is available from the Library of Congress.

10   9   8   7   6   5   4   3   2   1
15   14   13   12   11   10   09   08   07   06

Printed in China

In memory of
Ernest Warwick Dockrill
and
Mary Rita Hopkins

Contents

Contents

Contents

List of Abbreviations

ABM	Anti-Ballistic Missile system
AVRN	Army of the Republic of (South) Vietnam
CDU	Christian Democrats
CFE	Conventional Forces in Europe
CSCE	Conference on Security and Co-operation in Europe
DRV	Democratic Republic of (North) Vietnam
EDC	European Defence Community
FDP	Free Democrats
FNLA	National Front for the Liberation of Angola
GDR	German Democratic Republic
INF	Intermediate Nuclear Forces
MACV	Military Assistance Command, Vietnam
MAD	Mutual Assured Destruction
MBFR	Mutual and Balanced Force Reductions
MIRV	Multiple Independently Targetable Re-entry Vehicles
MLF	Multilateral Fleet
NATO	North Atlantic Treaty Organisation
NSC	National Security Council
PAVN	People's Army of (North) Vietnam
RVN	Republic of (South) Vietnam
SALT	Strategic Arms Limitation Treaty
SEATO	South East Asia Treaty Organisation
SPD	Social Democrats
START	Strategic Arms Reduction Treaty
SWAPO	South West Africa People's Organisation
UN	United Nations
UNITA	The Union for the Total Liberation of Angola

Editors' Preface

The Studies in European History series offers a guide to developments in a field of history that has become increasingly specialised with the sheer volume of new research and literature now produced. Each book has three main objectives. The primary purpose is to offer an informed assessment of opinion on a key episode or theme in European history. Second, each title presents a distinct interpretation and conclusions from someone who is closely involved with current debates in the field. Third, it provides students and teachers with a succinct introduction to the topic, with the essential information necessary to understand it and the literature being discussed. Equipped with an annotated bibliography and other aids to study, each book provides an ideal starting point to explore important events and processes that have shaped Europe's history to the present day.

Books in the series introduce students to historical approaches which in some cases are very new and which, in the normal course of things, would take many years to filter down to textbooks. By presenting history's cutting edge, we hope that the series will demonstrate some of the excitement that historians, like scientists, feel as they work on the frontiers of their subject. The series also has an important contribution to make in publicising what historians are doing, and making it accessible to students and scholars in this and related disciplines.

JOHN BREUILLY
JULIAN JACKSON
PETER H. WILSON

Preface

The first edition of *The Cold War* covered only the first two decades of the East–West confrontation. This new edition extends over the succeeding three decades so as to provide an account of the entire Cold War era. It now deals with the Vietnam War in its entirety and the process of East–West détente under Nixon and Ford. The 'New Cold War' period of the late 1970s and early 1980s gave way to a renewed East–West rapprochement under Gorbachev, the momentum of which eventually ended the Cold War with the collapse of the Soviet Union in 1991. This volume explains why the Cold War ended as it did and examines the roles of Gorbachev and Reagan in the process. The first edition was written just before the end of the Cold War, when there were few Soviet or Chinese sources. This new edition has benefited from the documents emerging from the Soviet and East European archives and, to a lesser extent, from Chinese archives. These materials have found a wider readership among Western scholars thanks to their translation by the Cold War International History Project in Washington. More documents from the communist powers need to appear, especially from China, to match the abundance of Western sources but we now have a solid documentary foundation for the Cold War era. Many excellent studies have been written using these sources and been utilised in this study.

Note on Chinese names. This book reflects the usage of the time it covers. Transliteration of Chinese characters changed from Wade-Giles to Pinyin Versions: Mao Tse-tung to Mao zedong; Chiang Kai-Shek to Jiang Jieshi; Peking to Beijing; Formosa to Taiwan.

Map 1   Europe
Adapted from: T.G. Paterson, J.G. Clifford and K. Hagen, *American Foreign Relations: A History Since 1895*, 4th edn (Lenington, Massachusetts, 1995), p. 278.

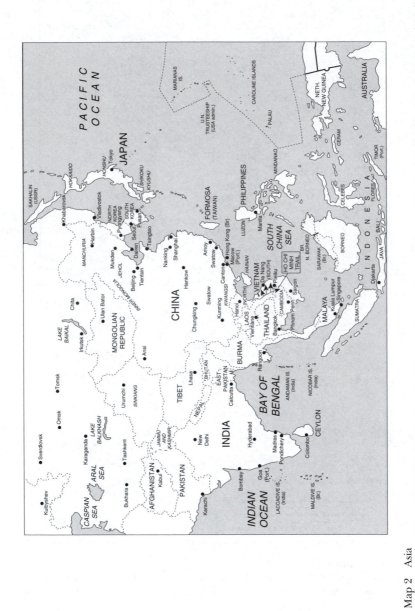

Map 2 Asia
Adapted from: Richard W. Leopdd, *The Growth of American Foreign Policy: A History* (New York: Alfred A Knopf, 1964), p. 764–765.

xiv

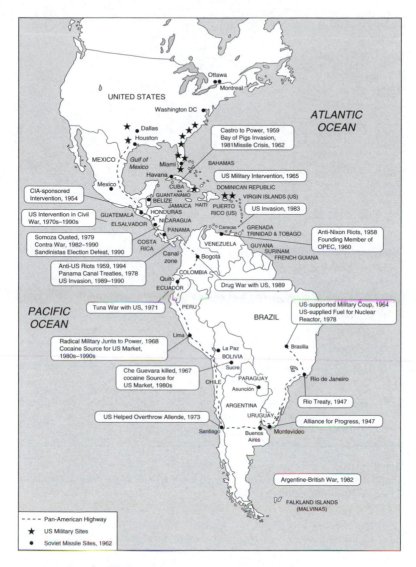

Map 3 US and Latin America
Adapted from: Antony Best et al., *International History of the Twentieth Century* (London: Routledge, 2004), p. 365.

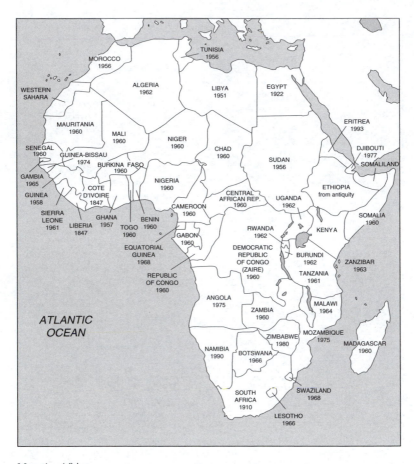

Map 4   Africa
Adapted from: Antony Best et al., *International History of the Twentieth Century*
(London: Routledge, 2004), p. 386.

Introduction

For nearly half a century after 1945 the Cold War dominated international relations. The Cold War has been defined as a state of extreme tension between the superpowers, stopping short of all-out war but characterised by mutual hostility and involvement in covert warfare and war by proxy as a means of upholding the interests of one against the other. It might not have become a 'hot' war but it was a dangerous era. Indeed, it remained 'cold' because the development of nuclear weapons had made resort to war a suicidal enterprise: both sides would be totally devastated by such an eventuality. The struggle between the two sides was accordingly pursued by indirect means, very often at considerable risk, and the resulting tensions ensured that both sides maintained a high and continuous state of readiness for war. The massive expenditures by both sides on research and development of nuclear arsenals and delivery vehicles led to a spiralling arms race which could, in turn, as a result of miscalculation by one side or the other, have resulted in a holocaust. There is a huge bibliography seeking to interpret and explain the origins and development of the 'Cold War'. Inevitably these interpretations have changed in response to the influence of contemporary developments on the writers. For the most part the writings of Western historians in the late 1940s and 1950s reflected the preoccupation of the governing elite with the evils of communism. US diplomats had experienced the menacing nature of the Soviet state at first hand during the 1930s and many of them had not been converted to a more favourable view during the high summer of Soviet–American friendship during the Second World War. Their warnings about Soviet malevolence in 1945 and 1946 coincided with the discovery by top American decision-makers in Washington that co-operation with the Soviet Union was likely to

1

prove more difficult than they had anticipated during that war. Memories of wartime obstructionism by Soviet bureaucrats and of their scant gratitude for American aid were rekindled after 1945, as the Soviets tenaciously clung to their notions of post-war security – notions which clashed with American expectations of continuing collaboration [46].

As the world plunged into the Cold War, American historians took up the theme of the fundamental antagonism of the communists for the capitalist system and, in the process, exaggerated the Soviet threat to the West, intensifying the apprehensions of a generation of American students and thus helping to fuel the anti-communist hysteria which gripped the United States in the early 1950s. The appeals for restraint by cooler heads, such as George Kennan, were ignored. US policy-makers and academics were deluged with a flood of information about Soviet intentions, all of which seemed to confirm their existing view of the sinister and dangerous nature of Soviet policy. In the same way, Soviet writers, most of whom were long schooled in the Leninist view that the capitalist system was fundamentally hostile to socialism, would have been unwise to voice contrary opinions while Stalin was closing off the Soviet Union from Western influences and consolidating his hold on the border states, especially as, in any case, American policy seemed to confirm their prejudices.

When Cold War tensions began to subside later, American historians turned against the prevailing orthodoxy. During the late 1960s and early 1970s Western interpretations of the Cold War were affected by the costly and seemingly endless conflict in Vietnam. A revisionist school of historians emerged, chiefly American, who tended to blame the United States for originating the Cold War and for extending it. Stalin was now seen as essentially a cautious and defensive leader, with the United States misinterpreting and overreacting to his efforts to protect Soviet security, thus making a tense situation even more dangerous. These writers argued that the rift between the two superpowers was the result of the ambitions of a United States which had grown rich and powerful during the Second World War and which, after 1945, wanted to extend its power throughout the world by the exercise of its immense financial strength. In order to achieve this ambition it sought overseas markets and investment opportunities. This capitalist imperative clashed with the insistence of the Soviet

Union on preserving its particular socio-economic system, much weakened by the destruction inflicted on the country during the Second World War. Thus the Soviet Union's policy towards the United States was dictated by the necessity of avoiding being overwhelmed by American capitalism, which would have turned the Soviet Union into a mere raw materials base for the West. The Cold War arose when the United States attempted to exercise its economic strength in Central and Eastern Europe, an area whose control by the Soviet Union was vital to Soviet security [55; 71; 115].

During the later 1970s, with the opening of United States archives to academic scrutiny, under the Freedom of Information Act, a new school of so-called post-Vietnam revisionists emerged. John Lewis Gaddis is a leading exponent of this school. It resulted in a more sophisticated analysis of the origins of the Cold War, which sought to demonstrate that the clash between the US and the Soviet Union arose from misunderstandings of each other's policies and was often the result of over-reaction by both sides to often defensive moves by the other [45]. Other American writers investigated more carefully available material on Soviet policy in these years – the input from Soviet historians has usually been both inadequate and affected by ideological considerations – only in the post-Cold War years were some Soviet archives opened to researchers. These American 'Sovietologists' demonstrated what was obvious to Western diplomats in Moscow at the time – that Stalin alone could never have controlled the Soviet Union completely after 1945. The complex society which Russia had become after the Second World War could not have been ruled single-handedly by one man [80]. Whole areas of internal policy were controlled by the bureaucracy with little, if any, reference to the Politburo. Nevertheless these writers admit that Stalin managed to keep a close watch on foreign policy decisions while his associates remained intimidated by him, and he was still capable of exerting his authority in matters of crucial importance to the Soviet Union. Even at the end of his life it is clear that he was meditating a purge of the other communist leaders. Thus, while these historians have drawn our attention to the difficulty of regarding the Soviet Union as a pure dictatorship in those years, it is still evident that Stalin, despite the struggles in which he had to engage, succeeded in maintaining his overall power in the Soviet Union, even if there were frequent fluctuations in foreign policy as a result [108].

In the same way Khrushchev's internal difficulties and his struggle with his political and military adversaries in the Soviet Union are now seen as more crucial to the changes of policy towards the West in the 1950s and early 1960s – a combination of bluster and threats mingled with appeals for peaceful co-existence – than Khrushchev's own mercurial temperament, although this must have had some effect [75]. Thus the Cold War in this more recent historiography was seen as a product of miscalculation rather than malevolence by both sides. However, in the last analysis Western writers saw the Soviet Union as the prime motivator: its suspicions and mistrust of the West condemned the world to a bi-polar struggle for power while the United States was criticised for over-reacting to Soviet actions. Since the fall of the Berlin Wall and the disintegration of the Soviet Union, many Soviet archives have been open to inspection by Russian and Western scholars. Many, of course, remain closed but what has been revealed so far in the many recent monographs and articles based on the Soviet archives have not greatly altered the previous interpretations of Soviet policy, although they have provided more detail and more background information about the way the policy was formulated.

Norman Graebner, a leading historian of the Cold War, has suggested that deeper causes than misunderstandings between the United States and the Soviet Union were responsible for the Cold War, and these lay deep within American history and tradition [51; 52]. Developments since 1945 can be ascribed, he believes, to the marriage of American idealistic universalism – that American values of liberty and constitutionalism have world-wide applicability – to the new-found military and material might of the United States. Graebner points out that this kind of universalism, as expressed in the Truman and Eisenhower Doctrines, was often not only repugnant to many of its intended beneficiaries who, with some justice, suspected that it was a cover behind which the United States was pursuing its own interests, but that even a powerful nation like the US was, in the last resort, incapable of imposing its will on them, as the Vietnam War demonstrated so starkly. The result, after 1975, was frustration and disillusionment, and a retreat from universalism. However, a recovery of

American self-confidence in the 1980s led to a new surge of 'Pax Americana'.

The so-called *realpolitik* school of historians of the Cold War – Graebner, Louis Hallé and Hans J. Morgenthau, although the latter is more a theorist of international relations than a historian – has either downgraded or dismissed altogether the importance of ideology as a factor in American and Soviet foreign policy. They consider ideology a mask behind which the two superpowers pursued their own selfish interests and a means of justifying their policies to the outside world. Thus these writers see little difference between the diplomatic manoeuvres of the nineteenth-century European states – German Chancellor Otto von Bismarck is seen as the most skilful practitioner – and the activities of the twentieth-century superpowers. They see ideology as merely an additional weapon in the diplomatic arsenal, a propaganda tool to rally their own people behind them, to undermine the will of the adversary's population and to appeal to the uncommitted elsewhere.

While there is some truth in this assumption, it is not of course the whole truth. Marxism–Leninism was the basic tenet of the Soviet state. It was regarded as the cornerstone of the organisation of the Soviet Union, and its teachings provided the goal towards which communists should strive. However cynical men like Malenkov and Khrushchev may have been in other respects, communism motivated them and they genuinely believed that its so-called blessings had universal application. In the same way, the liberal Christian and capitalist ideology of the United States is wholeheartedly accepted by most Americans and reinforces their patriotism and love of country. It was an inspiration to presidents from Truman and Eisenhower to Reagan and Bush who also believed in the universality of its appeal.

During the 1950s and 1960s the United States devoted considerable energies to promoting its anti-communist missionary zeal and in the process world tension increased rather than diminished. John Foster Dulles's frequent diatribes against the so-called world communist conspiracy suggested that no compromise was possible with the forces of evil. Later his bellicose language was matched by Khrushchev's own brand of sabre-rattling. While Eisenhower was slightly more flexible and was prepared to make a few harmless gestures of amiability towards Moscow, he also believed that a true meeting of minds between the United States and the Soviet Union was impossible while the Soviet regime survived in its existing form. In any case this indifference reflected the assumption that the United States was strong enough to act as the world's policeman and had no need of arms agreements or closer relations with the Soviet Union, even if these had been on offer.

John F. Kennedy was uniquely qualified to continue and extend Eisenhower's anti-communist crusade. Relatively young, arrogant and forceful, he claimed that his idealism was more sincere, purposeful and progressive than that of his complacent predecessor. In his speeches he extolled the American dream of liberty and prosperity as a universal goal. Critics continued to point out that the consequences seemed to be that the US supported dictatorial regimes like those of Syngman Rhee in South Korea and (until 1963) of Ngo Dinh Diem in South Vietnam, whose ideas about liberty and freedom were not founded in any way upon American precepts.

The Cuban missile crisis had the effect of increasing the already bounding confidence of the United States in its own destiny. President Johnson's decision to commit American air and ground forces to South Vietnam in 1965 reflected this vision of an all-powerful US actively combating the spread of communism and defending American values in the free world. The reality, of course, was more complicated. When the Vietnam intervention failed to achieve its purpose, President Nixon reduced the American commitment there and finally abandoned South Vietnam altogether. Nixon and his Secretary of State, Henry Kissinger, pursued a triangular diplomacy aimed at exploiting Sino-Soviet differences so as to create the opportunity for disengagement from Vietnam. They aimed at the normalisation of American relations with Communist China and *détente* with the Soviet Union. But the atmosphere of détente did not prevail. Many American conservatives in the 1970s reverted to ideological anti-communism and criticised Presidents Nixon and Ford and Kissinger, accusing them of weakening the US in comparison with the Soviet Union. Ronald Reagan was among the most vocal of these critics. So his presidency from 1981 focused on reversing what he saw as the Soviet Union taking advantage of the temporary weakness of the US after Vietnam to expand its armaments and extend its power and influence in the Third World. Reaganism represented a renewed

American determination to counter and overturn this communist challenge. Yet Reagan's term of office saw decisive changes that helped end the Cold War. Debate continues about the importance of his role as against that of the last Soviet leader, Mikhail Gorbachev, in hastening the close of East–West conflict.

1 Origins, 1917–1945

1917–1941

Antagonism had been inherent in the American–Soviet relationship since the Bolshevik Revolution of 1917. The two great continental states represented totally opposed ideologies: the United States embraced the values of liberal, capitalist democracy, while the Soviet Union was the first 'socialist republic', a communist dictatorship dedicated to spreading 'world revolution' by overthrowing the existing world order. These ideological differences were starkly revealed as the First World War ended in November 1918 and a peace conference, at which Russia was not represented, was convened in Paris in January 1919. United States war aims, as expressed in Woodrow Wilson's Fourteen Points speech of the previous year, envisaged a world based on the principle of national self-determination and a League of Nations which would replace the unstable pre-1914 system of alliances and balance of power politics. The Soviets, on the other hand, led by V.I. Lenin, insisted that the worldwide victory of the proletariat was the only basis for a peaceful world. Western assistance to anti-communist forces in Russia attempting to overthrow the Bolshevik regime in the early post-war years heightened the suspicions of the Soviet leadership about the implacable hostility of the capitalist states towards them, and about their determination to crush the new Soviet republic. Woodrow Wilson's vision of a world dedicated to the preservation of peace, in which the United States would play a major part, was destroyed when the United States Senate in 1920 repudiated the Treaty of Versailles with Germany, which the major allies had negotiated so laboriously in Paris in 1919. The League of Nations Covenant was an integral part of the Treaty and the Senate decision meant that the United States would not be involved in the organisation. Thereafter the United States retreated into isolationism. However, the mutual suspicion between the United States and the Soviet Union did not subside. The United States, angered by the Bolsheviks' repudiation of the Tsarist debts owed to the West, refused to recognise the Moscow regime, even after it became clear in 1920 that the Soviet Union would survive both internal and external threats to its existence.

Following the death of V.I. Lenin in 1924, a struggle for power between his heirs led to the emergence of Joseph V. Stalin as Soviet leader. Stalin was less interested than his rivals in exporting revolution and more concerned to build up the Soviet Union's industrial and military base in order that Russia might become the bastion of communism and, as such, able to resist aggression by the capitalist West. The gigantic sacrifices the industrialisation process imposed on the Soviet people and economy led to a preoccupation with internal affairs, just as the onset of the depression in the United States in 1929 had a similar effect in increasing isolationist sentiment there. However, Japanese aggression in Manchuria and China after 1931 prompted Stalin and the newly elected United States President, Franklin Delano Roosevelt, each increasingly concerned about the threat of a militarist Japan to their interests in Asia, to open diplomatic relations with each other in 1933. Stalin agreed to recognise the former Tsarist debts in return for a loan from the United States, but this agreement soon foundered on mutual disagreements about its terms. There was little meeting of minds, given their two different systems of government.

On paper the Soviet constitution which Stalin introduced in 1936 guaranteed the Soviet citizens' legal and democratic rights: in practice the Communist Party was supreme, with its powers vested in the party organs of the Politburo and the Secretariat, over which Stalin presided. The Party Congress met seldom, while the All Union Central Committee was a mere rubber stamp for decisions already reached. After Stalin's purges of his former colleagues and of the Red Army in the late 1930s, Stalin's will was unchallenged. These purges disgusted Soviet experts in the State Department and US diplomats in Moscow, such as George F. Kennan: men who were to emerge in senior positions in the State Department and the American diplomatic service during and after the Second World War with their suspicions of the Soviet Union undiminished. They were to exercise an important influence on American foreign policy during the early stages of the Cold War. American hostility towards the Soviet Union during the late 1930s was increased by the signature of the Non-Aggression Pact between the Soviet Union and Nazi Germany in August 1939. Stalin justified his alliance with Nazi Germany by pointing to the reluctance of Great Britain and France to join the Soviet Union in the 1930s in standing up to Hitler, preferring instead to appease Hitler, with the object, Stalin claimed, of encouraging Germany to turn on Russia. The Soviet Union would therefore remain neutral in this new 'capitalist war'.

American hostility towards the Soviet Union after 1919 was mild compared with the intensity of the fear and suspicion with which that country was regarded by Britain and France, particularly during the 1920s. These two democracies had taken the lead in organising Western assistance to the anticommunist ('White') forces during the civil war in Russia, when token forces of Anglo-French troops had been despatched to North Russia and the Crimea to fight alongside the Whites. Antagonism in the West towards the Bolsheviks had been provoked by Lenin's decision to withdraw Russia from the war with Germany and to sign a peace treaty with the Central Powers in the spring of 1918. The repudiation by the Bolsheviks of the debts owed to foreigners by the Tsarist regime had particularly hurt the French, who had invested large sums in Russia's industrialisation and rearmament programmes before 1914.

After 1918 London and Paris hoped that the Bolsheviks would be destroyed by their internal enemies and in the meantime refused to recognise the regime or allow it (or indeed any of the other contenders for power) to represent Russia at the Paris Peace Conference. Bolshevik propaganda and financial assistance were used to incite revolution amongst the working classes of Western Europe and this caused the ruling classes in the West considerable concern and anger [111]. Subsequent Soviet efforts to spread disaffection in India against British imperialism also made the establishment of stable relations between the Soviet Union and Britain extremely difficult, and indeed, towards the end of the 1920s, British military strategists were drawing up plans for a possible war with Soviet Russia on the north-west frontier of India.

Although the rise of Hitler's Germany after 1933 brought France and Soviet Russia together in a shaky alliance in 1935, the connection remained unpopular in France, and Paris refused to sign a military convention with its new ally. When the Soviet Union joined the League of Nations and began to call for collective action by the democratic states against fascism, many policy-makers in Western Europe mistrusted its motives, suspecting that this was a new Soviet ruse to project its influence and ideology into Europe. Britain distanced itself from these Soviet appeals for co-operation, preferring to seek agreement with Nazi Germany to preserve peace in Europe and only when this effort failed in 1939 did Britain join with France in attempting to negotiate a military convention with the Soviet Union. The failure of these talks, followed by the signature of the Nazi-Soviet pact in August 1939, convinced British leaders that their caution had been justified. The Soviet Union's seizure of part of Poland in October 1939, and later of the Baltic States and other border territories in the Balkans, and especially its attack upon Finland in the winter of 1939, were further serious blows to what little remaining credibility the Soviet Union possessed in London and Paris. Indeed, during the Soviet–Finnish war, there was talk in official circles of Anglo-French intervention to assist the Finns against the Soviets.

Thus, despite the dramatic events in the summer of 1941, with the Soviet Union now fighting Germany, a considerable fund of distrust of Soviet ambitions had been built up, particularly in London, during the inter-war period, and this was to resurface after 1945. Indeed, Winston Churchill, British Prime Minister from May 1940 to July 1945, had been the prime mover in organising Western intervention against the Bolsheviks in 1919, and in 1945 he repeatedly urged on an unresponsive Roosevelt and a wavering Truman a more vigorous Western reaction to Soviet challenges in Eastern Europe.

Soviet–American Relations during the Second World War, 1941–1945

When the Germans turned on their former ally and invaded the Soviet Union on 22 June 1941, Winston Churchill and Roosevelt insisted that Britain and the United States should supply the Soviet Union with munitions although their respective military chiefs did not think that the Red Army would survive for more than a few weeks. The two Western leaders believed that it was essential that the West should supply the Soviet Union with guns, armoured vehicles, aeroplanes and sophisticated military equipment of all kinds of which the Red Army was in critical need. If the Soviet Union collapsed, Nazi Germany would be able to devote all its efforts to subduing Britain and then, backed by captured Soviet raw materials and other resources, it would become a major threat to American security.

By September 1941 both Britain and the Soviet Union were receiving as much material support as the steadily reviving American industrial economy could supply, but the United States remained outside the conflict. While isolationism in the United States was slackening, Roosevelt realised that the American people were opposed to American involvement in another war. The Japanese attack on Pearl Harbor on 7 December 1941, followed by Hitler's declaration of war on the United States, finally brought the latter into the war as an ally of Britain and the Soviet Union against Germany. However, underlying tensions between these three great powers, while hidden from public view, did not diminish. The Soviet Union complained bitterly about the repeated Anglo-American delays in launching a second front – a cross-Channel invasion of France from Britain to relieve German pressure on the Soviet Union. Although there were important logistical and technical arguments against an early cross-Channel invasion, an associated factor in the minds of both Churchill and Roosevelt was the need to avoid heavy losses of American and British lives in a premature assault on German-occupied France. Stalin suspected that the two Western powers intended to let the Soviet Union suffer most of the human and material losses in the war against Germany, and he did not regard the Anglo-American invasions of North Africa and Southern Italy in 1942 and 1943 as substitutes for a full-scale Allied attack into the heartland of the Reich. For their part London and Washington feared that a beleaguered Stalin might make a separate peace with Germany.

By early 1942, when it became clear that, despite its immense losses, the Soviet Union would survive the German onslaught, Stalin exploited these Western fears of a German–Soviet separate peace by demanding Allied recognition of the territorial gains he had made as a result of the Nazi–Soviet pact. In 1944, as his victorious armies began to sweep across Central and Eastern

12

Europe, he pressed the Western powers to agree that the post-war governments of these countries should be pro-Soviet in orientation. Inevitably, since the area would be under Red Army occupation, communist parties would play a leading role in whatever governments were established. Stalin was determined that the region should never again become a conduit for German aggression against the Soviet Union [79].

Stalin's aims did not fit comfortably into Anglo-American notions about the post-war world. By 1944 the United States, having far outstripped Britain in military, economic and industrial strength, was the dominant partner in the alliance, and it fully intended to have a major voice in the post-war settlement. Roosevelt had not formulated a precisely defined post-war peace programme but had instead articulated a set of idealistic principles which were intended to unite both American and Allied opinion against fascism [25]. Although in 1941 Churchill and Stalin had associated themselves with Roosevelt's concept of a post-war world based on the rights of all peoples to self-determination, Stalin had no intention of letting such ideals affect his policy towards Eastern Europe, while Churchill had equally no intention of applying them to the British Empire.

Another strand in American thinking about the post-war period, and one which appealed particularly to the American Secretary of State, Cordell Hull, was that the post-war world economic order should be based on the principle of the open door to trade and investment. In Hull's view the rise of the aggressors in Asia and Europe had been primarily the result of the dislocation of the world economy after 1929, when tariff barriers had so diminished world trade that the most economically deprived, and yet vigorous, states like Germany and Japan had turned to overseas expansion for their economic salvation. Thus a renewed post-war slump could be avoided if all nations had equal access to world markets, supplies of raw materials and investment opportunities. As a result world trade would burgeon and all nations, rich and poor, would prosper, thus reducing the economic discontent and the gross inequalities which had provided fertile soil for fascism.

Revisionist American historians, in attempting to counter American accusations that the aggressive behaviour of the Soviet Union had been responsible for the Cold War, used the economic aspects of American planning for the post-war world as a means of laying the major part of the blame on the United States. As two writers of this school put it, 'essentially the United States' aim was to reconstitute the world so that American business could trade, operate and profit without restriction everywhere' [71:6]. They argued that the United States search for world economic domination after the war led to a collision with the Soviet Union, determined not to allow its war-weakened economy to be dominated by American big business. Thus, in this view, the ensuing deterioration in American–Soviet relations resulted from Soviet efforts to defend itself and its interests against American economic expansionism [71: 61].

It is true that American economists feared that the United States would face the same problems of reconversion to a peace economy as in 1919, and a world which was open to American exports would lessen the chance that its transition from war to peace would lead to heavy unemployment in the United States. But the revisionist theorists do not satisfactorily explain why increasingly tense Soviet–American relations after 1945 originated in Eastern Europe, an area which had attracted little American trade and investment before 1939 and was not likely to provide the United States with any greater opportunities after 1945 [91]. The revisionists also tend to dismiss as hypocrisy the very real vein of idealism which animated American conceptions of the post-war world, conceptions which were influenced as much by political as by economic considerations. There is little doubt that the United States did want to see a world reconstructed in its own image after the war, but this did not necessarily suggest the cynical motives the revisionists believe lay behind it. Roosevelt, a shrewd and pragmatic politician, recognised that American ideas about the post-war world would not necessarily be acceptable to the Soviet Union. They did not always appeal to the United States, closest ally, Great Britain. For instance, Churchill rejected Roosevelt's pressure for the decolonisation of the European empires in Asia after the war. Roosevelt feared that the differences between the expectations of his allies and those of American public opinion about the shape of the post-war world might become insurmountable. After the upsurge of internationalism which took place in the United States from 1941 onwards, selfish actions by his allies might lead to corresponding American disillusionment and a revival of the isolationism which, in Roosevelt's view, had done so much to encourage fascist aggression in the 1930s. Indeed, Roosevelt was so concerned to avoid the fate of Woodrow Wilson that he had discouraged talk of a new League after the war, but had emphasised instead a concept of 'Four Policemen' – China, the US, the Soviet Union and Britain – who would together maintain world peace. When it became clear that the American people wanted something more principled than a world dominated by the 'Big Four', Roosevelt had embraced the concept of a United Nations (UN) as a peacekeeping organisation. This would consist of a General Assembly of all non-fascist states, but the four-policemen concept would be retained in the Security Council of the great powers, who would exercise effective control of the organisation [25; 31].

Roosevelt attributed much of the American disillusionment with the post-1919 world to the immense gulf between Woodrow Wilson's vision of a just and stable world order and the selfish war aims of the victorious West European powers. This dichotomy contributed to American alienation from the peace settlements. Roosevelt was determined that the United States should not become involved in selfish territorial deals which had so disfigured the 1919 settlement and he tried to discourage Britain and the Soviet Union from entering into them. Roosevelt was, however, well aware of the Soviet Union's preoccupation with its security and of the reservations which Moscow and London entertained towards his principles.

He was not so concerned about Britain's opposition – its economic and financial plight resulting from its wartime sacrifices would make it dependent on the United States after the war. Roosevelt was convinced that post-war peace and stability hinged upon continued Soviet–American co-operation. His main argument was that Nazi Germany had brought the two countries together in uneasy alliance and, once this threat had been removed, there would be little to keep them united. Roosevelt was therefore determined to make the effort, chiefly by means of personal contacts with Stalin designed to convince the Soviet Union that the two powers could co-operate after the war. During his two wartime meetings with the Soviet leader at Teheran in 1943 and Yalta in 1945 he voiced his distrust of Britain and its imperialism to demonstrate to Stalin that there was no Anglo-American bloc ranged against the Soviet Union. At Teheran he hinted to Stalin that the United States would not oppose Poland's post-war frontiers being shifted

15

westward to give the Soviet Union Eastern Poland, with Poland securing as compensation the Oder-Neisse line at the expense of Germany. He also agreed that the Polish government should be reconstituted to exclude anti-Soviet elements. In return for these concessions he urged the Soviet leader to exercise discretion in handling the Poles so as not to antagonise Polish-American voters in the United States. While these undertakings were purely verbal, Stalin undoubtedly believed that he had been given a free hand in Eastern Europe. Conversely, Roosevelt was fully aware that once the Red Army had overrun Eastern Europe, the West would be in no position to influence Soviet behaviour, but he could hardly explain this to the American people. Hence, when Soviet actions in Eastern Europe made a mockery of the principle of self-determination, United States opinion turned against its former ally [45].

Churchill urged Roosevelt to agree to Anglo-American negotiations with Stalin to reach agreement on the limits to Soviet behaviour in Eastern Europe while the Soviet Union was still dependent on the West for assistance. Roosevelt, however, rejected such an Anglo-American front. Negotiations about territorial acquisitions and spheres of influence would lead to dissension between the Allies while the war was still to be won, and would cause an outcry in the United States if they became public knowledge. That was a major reason why Roosevelt did not welcome the so-called 'percentages' agreement which Churchill worked out with Stalin in Moscow in October 1944, giving the Soviets effective control over Romania, Bulgaria and Hungary, joint influence with Britain in Yugoslavia, and Britain freedom of action in Greece. In the early post-war years Stalin adhered to this agreement.

Roosevelt thus sought to defer detailed discussion of territorial and other questions until the war was over, since the United Nations would, he believed, provide a forum for the reconciliation of differences between the great powers. Unlike the post-1919 League of Nations, dominated by Britain and France, the United Nations would be a truly worldwide organisation, with the United States, the Soviet Union, Britain and China as founder members. Roosevelt's efforts to remain on good terms with the Soviet Union were assisted by Stalin's relaxation of strict party controls on Soviet culture after June 1941, by his emphasis on the traditional military and patriotic values of Russia and by his toleration of a limited religious revival. American commentators persuaded themselves that

16

these concessions heralded moves towards a more liberal and humane Russian society. Furthermore, the abolition in 1943 of the Communist International – the 'Comintern', an organisation of communist parties set up in March 1919, allegedly independent of Moscow and dedicated to spreading the communist message – signified to many Western observers that the Soviet Union was no longer interested in promoting international communism. Stalin's gestures were intended to stimulate Russian patriotic enthusiasm during a period of acute national emergency, and were not to lead to any far-reaching reform of the Soviet system. Indeed, the abolition of the Comintern had less to do with its effects on Western opinion and more to do with Stalin's desire to rein in the enthusiasm of European communist parties (who believed that the defeat of Germany and Italy would open the way to revolution in Europe) and bring them firmly under Moscow's control. Stalin had no wish to quarrel with the United States after the war and he was anxious to prevent communist coups in liberated countries which would alienate Western opinion [45; 79].

The Yalta Conference

On the brink of Germany's defeat, Churchill, Stalin and Roosevelt met for a second time at Yalta in the Crimea between 4 and 11 February 1945 to discuss the future of Europe. Roosevelt refused Churchill's request for a coordinated Anglo-American policy at the conference. Roosevelt persisted in his belief that personal discussion with Stalin would be more successful than if the Soviet leader were faced with an Anglo-American effort to 'gang up' against the Soviet Union.

As at Teheran, Roosevelt failed to make clear to Stalin how far he could pursue Soviet aims in Eastern Europe, and the vague wording of the agreements reached at Yalta on the future of the region again left Stalin with the impression that he was being given virtually a free hand. A casual remark by Roosevelt that he doubted that the American people would allow American troops to remain in occupation of Germany for more than two years after the war, and the obvious lack of any carefully thought out American proposal for the future of Germany, convinced Stalin that the United States was not greatly concerned about the fate of Central and Eastern Europe. The three powers merely accepted the agreements their officials had reached in 1944 on the military zones the three Allies would occupy in Germany after its surrender – although, on Churchill's insistence, France was also given a small zone. A four-power military council for Germany was set up in Berlin, which was also to be divided into four Allied military sectors. The future of Germany was left for determination by a future peace conference.

This division of Germany was not intended to be permanent. The powers agreed that Germany should be treated as an economic unit. The only post-war plan the Americans had formulated for the country was one drawn up in October 1944 by Henry Morgenthau, the Secretary of the Treasury, which proposed that Germany should be de-industrialised and turned into a pastoral community. Roosevelt and Churchill had assented to this plan at a time when anti-German feelings were running high but, by February 1945, they had come to the conclusion that it was impractical. Neither did Stalin have any definite policy about Germany, except to insist that the Russians should extract as much compensation as possible from the German economy for the damage the Nazis had inflicted on the Soviet Union. At Yalta the Soviets put forward a figure of $20 billion and demanded that the Soviet Union should receive priority in allocations of German capital equipment and payments in kind for a period of ten years. Since France and other countries occupied by Germany also put forward large reparation claims, this question was likely to cause considerable dissension. Neither the United States nor Great Britain were prepared to permit the Soviet Union and other claimants to seize Germany's resources, thus impairing its chances of future recovery, while they were forced, in order to keep the German people alive, to subsidise Germany's food and raw materials requirements. The conference postponed a decision on this issue by setting up a Reparation Commission to determine how much Germany should pay and in what form it should pay it – although the Soviet claim was accepted as the basis for discussion.

Stalin agreed that the Soviet Foreign Minister, V.M. Molotov, would attend a conference of the victorious powers at San Francisco in April 1945 to set up the United Nations Organisation. He insisted that each of the great powers represented on the executive organ of the United Nations, the Security Council, should have the right to veto any substantive resolution. Having ensured that the United Nations would not be able to thwart future Soviet policy, Stalin was quite willing to support the establishment of the United Nations, in which Roosevelt put so much faith, especially as, in return for Stalin's support, Roosevelt appeared to look sympathetically at Soviet demands elsewhere.

The three powers also reached a compromise over Poland. Shortly before the Yalta meeting Stalin had recognised a Soviet-backed Polish Communist Committee based at Lublin in Soviet-occupied Poland as the provisional government of Poland. Britain and the United States continued to recognise the Polish government-in-exile in London as the legitimate government, but this had shown itself too anti-Soviet and pro-Western for Stalin's taste. However, the two Western leaders avoided a confrontation over this issue by agreeing that the Lublin Committee was to form the nucleus of a Polish provisional government, with a few members of the London government allotted ministerial posts in this administration. Stalin also promised that free elections would be held in Poland after the war. Finally Stalin proposed that the Soviet Union annex Eastern Poland (with the addition of the former East Prussian port of Königsberg), while Poland was to receive compensation for this at the expense of Germany as far west as the Oder-Western Neisse rivers. Roosevelt, who had hinted at Teheran that he might approve such an arrangement, refused to agree publicly at Yalta to such an obvious breach of the principle of national self-determination. Churchill was even more distressed since, after all, Britain had ostensibly gone to war in 1939 to defend Poland's integrity but in practice there was little the Western leaders could do to prevent these changes since the Red Army was already in occupation of Eastern Poland, while the Poles were soon to seize the German territories allocated to them, expelling the German population as they did so.

Roosevelt was unwilling to risk a breach with Stalin over Poland, a country in which in any case he appeared to take little interest. On the other hand he was anxious to secure a Soviet promise to enter the war against Japan as soon as possible, as American military experts calculated that without Soviet assistance it would take as much as a further year of bloody struggle to subdue Japanese resistance. Soviet intervention would save many American lives and

Roosevelt was greatly relieved when Stalin agreed to declare war on Japan six weeks after the end of the European conflict. However, in return he demanded that the Soviet Union acquire the Japanese Kurile Islands, the southern half of Sakhalin Island, and railway, economic and port concessions in Chinese Manchuria. Roosevelt agreed to these transfers despite their apparent contradiction of Allied wartime pledges of no territorial aggrandisement.

Finally, Stalin signed a three-power Declaration on Liberated Europe which promised that Germany's former allies would be helped 'to solve by democratic means their pressing political and economic problems' and acknowledged 'the right of all peoples to choose the governments under which they lived'. This formula enabled Roosevelt to inform Congress that Yalta had confirmed the Atlantic Charter principles and gave the impression that Stalin was committed to working closely with the West. He did not, however, inform Congress of his agreement to the USSR's gains in the Far East, which led to much criticism when it was revealed later in the year: Roosevelt had also kept it secret from his closest advisers [39; 117].

Stalin had good reason to be satisfied with the results of the conference. In return for minor concessions – the acceptance of the United Nations and a future role for France in the councils of the great powers – he believed that the West had accepted Soviet control over Poland and Eastern Europe, although he recognised that this would have to be achieved behind a façade of self-determination. Roosevelt had said nothing at Yalta which disabused the Soviet leader of this impression. Stalin was willing to pay lip service to Western principles by encouraging the formation of so-called 'peoples' democracies' in Eastern Europe whereby communists formed coalition governments with anti-Nazi left and centrist parties. In countries under Red Army control real power of course rested with the communists although, for instance, in Czechoslovakia the collaboration between communist and non-communist parties was more genuine, given the considerable pro-Soviet sympathies of a population which felt itself betrayed by the West in 1938. Stalin's efforts to contain the revolutionary zeal of the communists were not accomplished without difficulty: the Yugoslav communist partisans, led by Marshal Tito, had liberated Yugoslavia largely by their own efforts and had no intention of sharing power with the discredited pro-royalist party, while in

20

China, American and Soviet efforts to persuade Mao Tse-tung's communists to collaborate with Chiang Kai-shek's nationalists failed completely. In France, Italy and Belgium communist leaders accepted ministerial posts in coalition governments [79; 80].

For his part, Stalin had refrained from interference in areas of Europe which the Western powers had liberated during the war and he anticipated similar Western restraint towards Soviet-occupied Eastern Europe. The Allies, after defeating Italy and finally forcing the German armies in the north to capitulate in 1945, had administered the country with little or no consultation with the Soviet Union and Stalin had not raised any serious objection. Furthermore Stalin had lived up to his November 1944 agreement with Churchill and had given no support to the Greek communist and left-wing forces in their bitter struggle with the British-backed royalist government (although Tito did provide some aid to the communists across the Yugoslav border). Stalin considered that in these circumstances he could anticipate a free hand in Poland and he did nothing to prevent the subsequent refusal of the communist Polish provisional government to admit representatives of the London Poles. United States diplomats in other Eastern European countries were at the same time warning Washington that communist excesses hardly suggested that the Soviet Union intended to live up to its Yalta promises. Events in Poland led to a stream of complaints from Churchill to Roosevelt about Soviet perfidy and, by the end of March, even Roosevelt began to contemplate taking a harder line towards Moscow.

President Harry Truman and the Soviet Union

His death on 12 April 1945 meant that historians can only speculate as to how Roosevelt would have handled the problem. His successor, Harry S. Truman, a former Senator from Missouri, who had been chosen as a compromise vice-presidential candidate in 1944, had been kept in complete ignorance by Roosevelt about foreign policy. Roosevelt's dual policy of public rhetoric about the principles governing the post-war world and his private assurances to Stalin that he recognised Soviet security concerns was not understood by Truman, who, while he promised to continue Roosevelt's policies, was unsure quite what these were.

21

His foreign policy advisers, men he had inherited from Roosevelt, were also divided about what course the new President should pursue. W. Averell Harriman, the United States ambassador to Moscow, who had returned home on hearing of Roosevelt's death, State Department officials, James F. Forrestal, the Navy Secretary, and Admiral William D. Leahy, the White House Chief of Staff, were all, in varying degrees, suspicious of Soviet policies and urged Truman to adopt a tough line towards Soviet violations of the Yalta accords. Henry L. Stimson, the War Secretary, Joseph E. Davies, a former pro-Soviet ambassador to Moscow, and General George C. Marshall, the Army Chief of Staff, pressed Truman on the other hand not to jeopardise the long-term prospects for Soviet–American co-operation for the sake of relatively minor Soviet transgressions in Eastern Europe, an area of little interest to the United States and where it was in any case powerless to influence the course of events. From London Truman was bombarded with telegrams from Churchill advocating a firm Anglo-American stand against the Soviet Union. Faced with this conflicting advice, Truman wavered. He was unwilling to adopt some of Churchill's more extreme suggestions, such as ordering Anglo-American forces to liberate Prague before the Russians arrived there, in order to prevent the communisation of Czechoslovakia. However, the President did remonstrate angrily with Molotov over Soviet violations of the Yalta agreements on Poland when the Soviet Foreign Minister visited Washington on 23 April on his way to the San Francisco Conference.

Truman soon realised that angry exchanges with Molotov were self-defeating, and by May he had reverted to Roosevelt's policy of conciliation. He believed that a direct appeal to Stalin about Poland over the heads of the supposedly hard-line Molotov and the Politburo might have more effect in changing Soviet policy. He sent Harry Hopkins, a close intimate of Roosevelt, who had used him as his personal emissary to Stalin during the war, to Moscow (26 May–6 June) to suggest to the Soviet leader a Big Three meeting in the early summer, and also to reach a compromise over the vexed Polish question. This direct approach appeared to work: Stalin accepted a summit, agreed that the non-communist leaders would be given places in the Polish provisional government (which took place on 21 June), repeated his Yalta promise of free elections in Poland and of Soviet entry into the war against Japan early in August. Churchill was irritated by Truman's *volte face* but had no alternative but to accept the results of the Hopkins mission and agree that the new Polish government should be recognised by the West once it had been reconstituted.

Despite this improvement in the atmosphere Truman remained at heart suspicious of Soviet policy, while Stalin, who had believed that he could work with Roosevelt, regarded Truman as an unknown quantity whose conduct so far towards the Soviet Union had been inconsistent. Truman's dilemma was that, given the rapid rundown in the numbers of American troops in Europe after Germany's surrender (some were transferred to the Far East, while others were being demobilised as quickly as possible to meet the growing clamour in the United States 'to bring the boys home'), the United States would soon have only a limited physical presence in Europe with which to back up its diplomacy [39; 45].

In these circumstances the only leverage available to the United States was its financial strength. In 1944 the American Treasury proposed that the United States offer the Soviet Union a loan to assist its post-war recovery and as evidence that the United States sought good relations with Moscow. Stalin and Molotov expressed interest, and it also appealed to American business, attracted by the possibility that Soviet purchases of American industrial plant and the ensuing recovery of the Soviet economy would offer opportunities for expanded American trade in the Soviet Union at a time when economists were predicting a post-war US slump. After he became President, Truman's advisers suggested that this loan could be used to secure Soviet promises of good behaviour in Eastern Europe. Molotov's repeated suggestions for negotiations about a loan were either ignored or were answered by hints from Harriman that political conditions might be attached to it. American evasiveness on the subject and such attempts at blackmail increased Stalin's growing suspicion of Truman. A sudden end of lend-lease supplies on 7 May 1945, a result of Congressional pressure after the end of the war in Europe (supplies for the Far East continued until August), was bound to fuel Stalin's doubts, although it affected Great Britain as much as it did the Soviet Union. The loan scheme lapsed in the summer of 1945 [90]. However, a further means of influencing Soviet behaviour emerged on 25 April 1945 when Stimson acquainted Truman with the closely guarded secret of the Manhattan Project – the development, during the war, of the atomic bomb by a team of American, British and Canadian scientists – which was now approaching fruition. This was successfully tested in New Mexico in mid-July and the War Secretary expected to have at least two bombs available for use against Japan. Gar Alperovitz [3] has suggested that Truman's major preoccupation during the summer of 1945 was not the final defeat of Japan but the use of American possession of the bomb as a means of coercing the Soviet Union into adopting American policies in Eastern Europe and elsewhere. The sole motive for exploding the bombs on Japan, according to Alperovitz, was not to force the Japanese into surrender – he claims they were on the verge of defeat in any case – but to impress the Soviet Union with American possession of a weapon of such awesome power. This is a grotesque exaggeration. Although in hindsight it is true that the US overestimated Japanese strength in early 1945, uppermost in Truman's mind at that time was that the use of the bomb would save countless American lives by forcing Japan into precipitate surrender.

The Japanese government had already put out peace feelers but it was doubted in Washington that that government was master in its own house. Moreover, no one could be sure in the spring of 1945 that the A-bomb would work, and Soviet intervention in the Far East was still considered crucial. However, undoubtedly some of Truman's advisers did think that the bomb would give the United States some bargaining strength in dealing with the Soviet Union. Truman's guarded hint to Stalin at the Potsdam Conference in July 1945 that the United States had successfully tested a weapon of great destructive power, was hardly likely to impress Stalin, whose non-committal reply concealed the fact that Soviet spies in the Western intelligence and scientific communities were keeping Moscow fully informed of the progress of the project. On returning to Moscow Stalin ordered the stepping up of Soviet efforts to produce a Russian nuclear weapon on which work had begun in 1942 [122]. United States employment of the A-bombs against the Japanese cities of Hiroshima and Nagasaki on 6 and 9 August 1945, which was followed by the Japanese surrender on the 15th, did not appear to have any effect on the course of Soviet policy. The Red Army entered the war as promised on 8 August and speedily overran Japanese positions in Manchuria. The Americans soon realised that their possession of the A-bomb gave them little diplomatic leverage to influence Soviet policy [77].

The Potsdam Conference and After, July–December 1945

The Potsdam Conference of the three great powers (17 July–1 August 1945) did not produce any major constructive agreement but it did conceal temporarily the growing divergence between East and West [117]. A reparations agreement was reached designed to reduce Soviet claims to German industrial capital in the three Western zones. Each occupying power was allowed to extract reparations freely from its own zone, while the Soviet Union was authorised to take 10 per cent from the Western zones and a further 15 per cent provided that this was matched by supplies of food and raw materials from the Soviet zone. The Soviets again promised free elections in Poland. The United States finally accepted the Oder-Western Neisse line as Poland's future Western frontier. Substantive issues, such as the long-term future of Germany and peace treaties with Germany's former European allies (eventually signed in 1946) were referred to future meetings of the foreign ministers of the great powers for resolution.

Molotov demanded that the Montreux Convention, which restricted the passage of non-Turkish military vessels through the Dardanelles, should be scrapped and Soviet and other Black Sea countries should be allowed to use the Straits freely in future, while a joint Soviet–Turkish administration should replace the international regime of the Straits. Churchill had intimated in 1944, and again at Yalta, that the Straits regime might be altered in favour of Soviet Russia as Turkey had refused to join the Allies against Germany (it did not declare war until April 1945). He now regretted his premature enthusiasm, especially as Molotov linked his demands with a call for restoration to the Soviet Union of Turkish territory in the border provinces of Kars and Ardahan, ceded by the Soviet Republic to Turkey in 1921, and later pressed for Soviet naval bases in the Straits. These far-reaching demands only increased Western suspicions of Soviet policy towards Turkey. They were referred to the foreign ministers [40; 117].

The problems of Italy and Romania were also aired at Potsdam, without any definite conclusion being reached. Both countries had switched sides during the war – Italy, after the overthrow of Mussolini in 1943 and the occupation of Southern Italy by the Western Allies, while Romania had been forced to declare war on Germany after the Red Army had entered the country in the following year. Both, however, were still regarded by the Allies as ex-enemy states.

Italy was governed largely by the British and American occupying forces through an Allied Control Commission, on which the Soviet Union had an advisory role, although in practice its presence was ignored. At the end of 1944 the Soviet Deputy Foreign Minister, Andrei Vyshinsky, visited Italy and helped to re-establish there a strong Communist Party, in the hope that the party would dominate a future Italian government when the constitution was restored. Beyond that, Stalin's Italian policy was obscure. Although Molotov protested at Potsdam about the Soviet Union's exclusion from the decision-making process in Italy, he did not press the matter. At the subsequent London Conference of Foreign Ministers he put forward a demand for $100 million in reparations from Italy, but Truman refused to lend Italy the money and the war-torn Italian economy was too impoverished to pay and the matter lapsed. Stalin was forced to move circumspectly – Yugoslavia wanted to annex Trieste, Italian since 1919, and defended in 1945 by Anglo-American troops. Stalin did not want to offend Tito by showing any support for Italy in the region. Italy remained in the Western camp after 1945, a result of the successful Allied defence of Trieste and generous American economic assistance.

Stalin used the West's refusal to allow the Soviet Union a voice in Italy to deny the Western Allies a say in the Control Commissions in Bulgaria, Hungary and Romania. In February 1945 Vyshinsky turned up in Bucharest and ordered King Michael to appoint a new pro-Soviet government dominated by the Communist Party. He warned the king that failure to do so might lead to the end of Romania's existence as an independent power and, on leaving, slammed the door so hard that the surrounding plaster cracked. In August the king tried to dismiss this government, invoking the Declaration on Liberated Europe and appealing to Britain and the United States for support. The West did nothing – Britain had no desire to disturb the 1944 percentages agreement with Stalin and risk Soviet interference in Greece, while Truman was indifferent to the question. In February 1946 the government was slightly enlarged by the addition of a few liberal politicians and, in return, the West agreed to recognise this new government. The change was purely cosmetic: the king was forced eventually to abdicate and the communists took over the country completely [80;85].

During the conference Churchill and the British Foreign Secretary, Anthony Eden, were replaced by Clement Attlee and Ernest Bevin respectively as a result of the Labour Party's victory in the British general election in late July 1945. A number of the newly elected Labour Members of Parliament had been pro-communist in the 1930s, while John Strachey, a junior Air Minister, had been a Communist Party member before the war. Some left-wing MPs pressed the new government to renounce its ties with capitalist United States and throw in its lot with socialist Russia, but these were in the minority. In any case Attlee and Bevin were men of a different stamp. Neither shared the pro-communist or wartime sentimentality towards the Soviet Union of some of their supporters, although they made some half-hearted attempts to keep the wartime friendship with the Soviet Union alive. Although the Labour Party election manifesto attacked the anti-Soviet foreign policy of the Conservatives before 1939 and called for the continuation of the alliances with the United States and the Soviet Union into the peace, Attlee and Bevin had come to the conclusion that the Soviet Union was an imperialist power whose ambitions threatened the independence of Western Europe.

Publicly Bevin found it politically expedient to declare that a Labour government was much better placed than a Conservative one to work with Moscow but privately, as a former trade union leader and wartime Minister of Labour, he was well acquainted with the machinations and ambitions of domestic communists. Bevin's experiences with the intransigence of Molotov and other Soviet negotiators at Potsdam and later meetings convinced him that his assumptions about Soviet malevolence had been correct: he became as suspicious of Soviet policy as Churchill had been [20].

East–West relations experienced further deterioration during the autumn and winter of 1945 as the Soviet Union ignored Western protests about the ill-treatment of non-communist parties in Eastern Europe. The first post-war meeting of the Council of

Foreign Ministers in London in September was the scene of angry accusations and counteraccusations. Molotov alleged British atrocities against Greek communists: Bevin condemned Soviet actions in Eastern Europe. The Soviets demanded a voice in the Allied occupation regimes in Italy and Japan, renewed their calls for the revision of the Montreux Convention and put forward a claim to a share in the trusteeship of Italy's former North African colony, Libya. Nor could any agreement be reached about the future of Germany – each side feared that a reunited Germany would fall under the other's influence. The occupation authorities had already started to treat their respective zones as their own separate satrapies, rendering the Potsdam agreement a dead letter. Indeed, the Yalta reparation accords hastened this tendency, as the Soviet Union began to extract the major share of its reparations claims from its own zone.

However, Truman's new Secretary of State, James F. Byrnes, still hoped for an agreement with the Soviet Union. Indeed Byrnes, whose reputation within the United States had been built up as a domestic conciliator, and who had been one of the two chief contenders for the vice-presidential nomination at the Democratic Party Convention in 1944 (from which Truman had emerged as the nominee), was convinced that he could achieve a working relationship with the Soviet Union by direct talks with the Soviet leaders. It was by now clear that American possession of the atomic bomb had had no impact on Soviet policy – if anything Molotov was even more obstinate at the London Conference than before. The Soviet demands in Turkey and Libya were put forward either as bargaining counters or to test Western will, but the Soviet Union also calculated that, since the United States was expanding its power worldwide, with bases in the Philippines and Japan, and had taken over Japan's former Pacific Island trusteeships in 1945, the Soviet Union, as a co-victor, had the right to achieve Russia's long-held ambition to secure unimpeded access to the Mediterranean. To the West, however, its demands appeared to be exorbitant, and they were bound to increase British anxiety about Soviet intentions in the Middle East and the Mediterranean, still a British preserve. Byrnes even suspected that the demand for a share in Libya's administration was part of a Soviet design to dominate Africa, and particularly the Belgian Congo, at that time the major source of the United States uranium supply [77].

Soviet leaders were more concerned with the immense problems of trying to recover from the effects of war and occupation, with resources inadequate to the task, than with foreign policy issues. Moreover, the pressures of war had led to the rise of the Red Army, which had won much prestige in the Soviet Union as a result of its victories over Germany, of the heavy industrial sector under G.M. Malenkov, which had been expanded enormously to meet the needs of the war, and of the political police (the Narodnyi Kommissariat Vnutrennikh Del (People's Commissariat of Internal Affairs) NKVD/Komitet Gosudarstvennoy Bezopasnosti (Committee of State Security) KGB) under L.B. Beria, which had accumulated vast powers during the war. Stalin feared that these powerful interests might challenge his authority, especially as the war had led to the weakening of Communist Party controls. In 1945 Stalin charged A.A. Zhdanov, a party activist and theoretician, with the task of reviving the influence of the party and countering the rising power of the military and industrial sectors [80]. Zhdanov was 'responsible for shaping a Cold War mentality inside the Soviet Union as well as for Communist followers and sympathisers all over the world' [122: 112].

These internal struggles, together with Stalin's fears of a new war, this time with the United States, were responsible for the cautious nature of his foreign policy, willing to test Western positions, yet receding if he met resistance, insisting on the Soviet Union's rights, yet uncertain of how to achieve them. Molotov's stubborn behaviour at the London Conference demonstrated the Soviet Union's determination to be treated as an equal by the West, and was designed to show that it was not to be overawed by the American monopoly of the atomic bomb [80].

However, the Soviet Union remained willing to take advantage of a more conciliatory approach, especially if this implied a rift in the Anglo-American relationship. Molotov accepted with alacrity a proposal by Byrnes that the three foreign ministers should meet in Moscow in December 1945. Britain was not consulted in advance about this initiative; plainly Byrnes hoped to reach agreement directly with Stalin and Molotov in Moscow. Bevin had no alternative but to attend the conference despite an earlier threat that he would stay away. At Moscow, after Byrnes had spoken to Stalin, the Soviet Union agreed that a Four-Power Control

Commission should be sent to Romania to ensure non-communist representation in its government, while non-communists would be given posts in the Bulgarian government. In return, the United States agreed to set up an Allied Council in Tokyo to make suggestions to General MacArthur, the United States Supreme Commander in Japan, and virtual ruler of the country, about the occupation regime there. Finally it was agreed that the Council of Foreign Ministers would meet in the spring of 1946 to draw up peace treaties with Germany's former European allies.

These mutual concessions were purely cosmetic: the Western powers would continue to have as little influence in internal political arrangements in Romania as the Allied Council would have in Tokyo. Nevertheless the Moscow Conference led to a temporary thaw in American–Soviet relations. While determined to maintain Soviet control in Eastern Europe, Stalin had demonstrated a willingness to accept a façade of Allied co-operation in the area. Nor was Truman willing to consider a complete breach with the Soviet Union while there remained a chance, however slender, of a deal, despite his complaints that Byrnes had made too many concessions to the Soviet Union in Moscow. He was becoming increasingly aware that the public mood in the United States was beginning to turn against the Soviet Union, although it would not become completely anti-Soviet until the end of the following year. In November 1946 the Republicans, in the mid-term elections, gained control of both houses of Congress for the first time in eighteen years. Domestic considerations were the main factors in this victory, but nevertheless Republican Senators, such as former isolationist Arthur H. Vandenberg of Michigan, the Republican leader in the Senate, were becoming increasingly vocal in their attacks on Byrnes's alleged 'appeasement' of Moscow. While Truman was certainly irritated by Byrnes's failure to keep him properly informed about his initiatives in Moscow, all this did not mark a clear parting of the ways between East and West.

Conclusion

The competing ideologies of capitalism and communism, the Soviet repudiation of the former Tsarist debts and American intervention in the Russian Civil War resulted in a climate of suspicion and hostility between the United States and the Soviet Union which failed to dissipate even when the United States recognised the Soviet Union in 1933. Inevitably the Soviet Union's alignment with Nazi Germany in 1939–1941 further antagonised the United States. However, the entry of both countries into the war against Germany in 1941 led to nearly four years of often uneasy collaboration against a common enemy. With the defeat of Germany and later Japan in 1945 both the United States and the Soviet Union hoped to continue their war time collaboration in order to maintain world peace and stability, in America's case, through a new world organisation, the United Nations. In early 1945 the Big Three, Roosevelt, Churchill and Stalin, managed to reach a shaky agreement on the future of Germany and Eastern Europe, but with Roosevelt's death the new President, Harry Truman, became suspicious of Soviet policy, particularly towards the Eastern European countries, now occupied by the Red Army. However, at the Potsdam Conference the three powers managed to paper over the cracks and produce an agreement which virtually confirmed the Yalta settlement, with Truman's confidence buoyed up by news of the American explosion of the atomic bomb. But when the three foreign ministers met in London in September for detailed negotiations over the principles reached at Potsdam, Molotov proved to be unyielding in his determination to secure Moscow's desiderata. The conference broke up without agreement and it seemed that East–West relations would plunge into acrimony. James Byrnes, Truman's new Secretary of State, hoped to avert a breach between the two sides by calling for a new Conference of Foreign Ministers in Moscow in December 1945, which managed to achieve a temporary *modus vivendi*. Republican sentiment in the United States was outraged by what it regarded as Byrnes' sell-out at Moscow, particularly in Eastern Europe, while Truman was annoyed by Byrnes' failure to keep him fully informed about the progress of the conference. Much would now depend on Stalin's view of future Soviet policy and on Truman's reaction to any real or alleged Soviet attempt to alter the existing status quo.

2 The Cold War Emerges, 1946–1952

Developments in 1946

The post-Moscow Conference thaw was short-lived. During 1946 there was a definite hardening of relations between the Soviet Union and the United States. By the following year a 'Cold War' had broken out which was to become the characteristic feature of East–West relations for the next two decades. The 'Cold War' was a state of continuing hostility and tension between the two world power blocs led by the United States and the Soviet Union. Before the advent of nuclear weapons the outcome of the bitter disputes between East and West, which spread from Europe to the Middle and Far East, would have been a major war. The possession of nuclear weapons of ever increasing and formidable power, and the appalling consequences of their use, did impose some restraint on the leaders of each side in their dealings with the other but, during the many confrontations between the two sides after 1946, the slightest miscalculation or overreaction might well have led to catastrophe. The enormous power of the hydrogen bomb, which both sides developed in the early 1950s, imposed even greater caution on them, but even before 1949, when the United States alone possessed the atomic bomb, Truman was as reluctant to contemplate its use as Stalin was to provoke it.

Speeches by Stalin and other Soviet leaders in February 1946 warned the Soviet people that they were still threatened by capitalist encirclement and accused Western 'imperialists' of encouraging the formation of an anti-Soviet bloc. However, the main purpose of the speeches was to prepare the Soviet people for the heavy sacrifices which would result from the new Five Year Plans for the rebuilding of heavy industry and of Soviet military strength. Furthermore, Molotov distinguished between the majority of peace-loving peoples of the world and the small group of reactionary elements in the West who sought renewed conflict – a hint that, if the peaceful majority exerted itself, co-existence was still possible [80].

Neither side had any real reason to fear the other in 1946. American army strength by March 1946 had fallen to 400,000 from a peak of 3.5 million in May 1945. The United States lacked sufficient atomic bombs to inflict a decisive blow on the Soviet Union. In any case, despite a marked decline in earlier pro-Soviet sentiment, the American people were unlikely to support a new conflict so soon after the end of the Second World War. American intelligence was well aware that the devastation inflicted on the Soviet economy by four years of ruinous war made it impossible for it to contemplate fresh hostilities: nor of course did Stalin seek a conflict. American attention focused more on the dangers posed by the strong communist parties in Western Europe, which thrived on conditions of acute economic and political instability. Some alarm was expressed at the presence of twenty Red Army divisions in Central Europe at a time when Western Europe's defences barely existed. Total Red Army strength was put at about 2.5 million in 1946. This was an exaggeration: the Soviet Union had also demobilised rapidly after 1945 in order to release manpower for industrial reconstruction, and the size and strength of each Red Army division was overestimated, as American analysts recognised later [118].

That United States opinion was not yet prepared to regard the Soviet Union as an implacable enemy was shown by the hostile reception in the United States of a speech by Winston Churchill, now leader of the British opposition, at Fulton, Missouri, on 5 March 1946, in which he talked of an 'iron curtain' having 'descended across the Continent [of Europe] from Stettin in the Baltic to Trieste in the Adriatic' and appealed for a renewal of the wartime Anglo-American alliance as a means of deterring Soviet expansionism. Truman, who had read the speech prior to its delivery, and was present at the address, subsequently disassociated himself from it [58]. Some of the protests were the product of suspicions that Churchill sought United States assistance to maintain the British Empire, while British efforts to deal even-handedly between the Arabs and Jews in the strife-torn British-mandated territory of Palestine created even further hostility towards London in the United States, where the powerful Jewish lobby accused the British of favouring the Arab cause. In December 1945 much bitterness was occasioned in Britain over negotiations for a much needed American loan of $3.75 billion. The terms of this loan were not onerous, but one of the conditions was that Britain should abolish commonwealth preferences and restore sterling to full convertibility by 1947, thus encouraging the expansion of American controls over Britain and its empire. This led to angry protests from both right- and left-wing MPs in the House of Commons about the implications for British interests and sovereignty of such a clause. The Americans also began to recede from Roosevelt's wartime pledge that Britain and Canada should receive full information about America's atomic programme after the war. In 1946 the McMahon Act resulted in a permanent ban on such information. From 1946 the British began to develop their own atomic bomb [8; 13; 20].

However, the steady deterioration in Soviet–American relations overshadowed these Anglo-American quarrels. In Germany mounting American irritation with Soviet and French reparations seizures in the United States zone led the United States army to suspend Soviet reparations deliveries on 3 May. The transfer of German industrial plant to the East threatened to wreck the economy of West Germany completely. Foreign Ministers Conferences in April, June and July 1946 deadlocked over the future of Germany. The West suspected correctly that the Soviets only wanted a unified Germany if it was under communist domination. The Soviets accused the United States of seeking a Germany tied economically and militarily to the West. There were endless arguments about the levels of industrial production Germany should be permitted to achieve, with the Soviet Union and France (who both had good reasons to fear a resurgent Germany) pressing for the pegging of German steel and other industrial production at a low level to prevent the revival of a German armaments industry. They also called for Franco-Soviet participation in an international authority to control the Ruhr, Germany's main industrial base. By 1946 Britain and the United States had concluded that the economic recovery of Western Europe as a whole depended on the rehabilitation of the German industries. While they were willing to provide safeguards against the re-emergence of a German military threat, including a twenty five-year, four-power treaty to guarantee the disarmament of the country (which the Soviets rejected), they opposed efforts to impose harsh controls on Germany's peaceful economic revival. The division of Germany into two hostile camps became more marked as both sides began to encourage the revival of German political parties on a local level in their zones. In East Germany the non-communist socialist party was merged into a communist front organisation (the Socialist Unity Party). Separatist tendencies in the West were enhanced when, on 6 September 1946, in a speech at Stuttgart, Byrnes reassured his German audience that the United States would not withdraw its occupation forces from West Germany in the foreseeable future. He stated that the United States would continue to support the reunification of Germany. If this should prove impossible, Washington intended to encourage the revival of the West German economy. Then, on 1 January 1947, Britain, economically exhausted and unable to continue to bear alone the burden of sustaining its zone, agreed to merge it with the American zone.

Events outside Europe created additional tensions. In 1942 the Soviet Union had occupied north Iran, and Britain the south, in order to prevent crucial Iranian oil resources falling to the Nazis, and to render it secure as an overland route for the passage of lend-lease supplies to the Soviet Union. Both powers had promised to withdraw their troops six months after the end of the war. On 15 March 1946 the British duly withdrew their forces but the Red Army in the north showed no sign of following suit. There were fears that the Soviet Union sought to annex the Iranian province of Azerbaijan and there were ominous reports of Soviet troop movement along the borders of Iran. The Soviet Union now began to demand that Teheran agree to grant Soviet agencies oil concessions in the north. Undoubtedly Stalin overplayed his hand. The Iranian government was not ill-disposed towards the Soviet Union, while Moscow felt that it had as much right to oil concessions in the north as Britain had to its valuable oil fields in the south. But the threatening behaviour of the Soviet Union led the State Department to suspect that the Russians were seeking to dominate Iran. Moreover, the United States was no longer self-sufficient in oil and insisted that the oil reserves of the Middle

East must be kept out of hostile control. Byrnes, now converted by Truman and Republican leaders to a hard line, made a fuss about the Soviet actions in both the United Nations and in protest notes to Moscow. Finally the Soviet Union withdrew its troops from North Iran in May, having extracted oil concessions from the Iranian government (which were subsequently repudiated by the Iranian Parliament) and restored Azerbaijan to full Iranian sovereignty. Truman was now convinced that a policy of firmness towards the Soviet Union paid dividends, while Soviet probing for advantage in Iran reinforced his suspicions of their motives [73].

Mutual suspicions also wrecked efforts to reach East–West agreement on the control of the atomic bomb. In 1945 Stimson, the War Secretary, had urged Truman to place the atomic secret under joint Soviet–American control. He argued that the Soviets were bound eventually to develop their own bomb: it would be better to anticipate the ending of the American monopoly by an early international agreement to neutralise this devastating weapon. A United States plan (the so-called Baruch plan) to place atomic raw materials and their inspection under a United Nations control agency, which would not be subject to the veto, foundered on the Soviet accusation that it would be prevented from developing its own nuclear capability, and its territory subjected to inspection, while the United States would retain its monopoly over the bomb during the formative years of the agency. A Soviet proposal to ban the production of nuclear weapons and the destruction of existing stockpiles was rejected by the United States. This debate, which took place during late 1946 in the newly created United Nations Atomic Energy Commission, was the precursor of long and futile East–West disarmament negotiations in which propaganda and Cold War rhetoric replaced any meaningful search for arms control [60; 78].

Hard-line elements in the American nuclear and military establishments were opposed to any tampering with their nuclear monopoly. They believed that even if Soviet scientists knew how to produce atomic bombs, American control of the world's main uranium deposits in the Belgian Congo, together with the Soviet Union's lack of technological expertise and of the expensive facilities needed to manufacture them, would retard a Soviet bomb for years. Truman accepted these arguments; the more so as he no longer felt it was possible to trust the Soviet Union.

The Truman Doctrine and the Marshall Plan

In 1947 Truman inaugurated the 'containment' of Soviet expansionism and ended the hesitancy which had characterised American policy towards the Soviet Union since 1945. Those Cabinet members who continued to believe that compromise was possible were eased out of office. Such was the fate of Henry A. Wallace, a former Vice-President and now Commerce Secretary, who was forced to resign in September 1946, after a speech in New York in which he called for a renewed effort to achieve a Soviet–American agreement. James Byrnes, whom Truman considered too soft towards the Soviet Union, was replaced as Secretary of State in January 1947 by General George C. Marshall, the wartime Army Chief of Staff. Moreover, political considerations forced Truman to conclude that there could be no meaningful negotiations with the Soviet Union in 1947. After the November 1946 Republican victories in the Congressional elections, Truman's legislation was dependent on the votes of staunchly anti-communist Republicans who, paradoxically, sought to curb government expenditure and lower taxation. Truman would have to dwell upon Soviet hostility if he was to persuade these senators to vote extra money for defence and overseas expenditures. The most dramatic indication of the Truman administration's new hard-line policy towards communism was its decision to take over Britain's responsibilities for meeting the military costs of the Greek government's military campaign against Greek communist insurgents. The government, despite this aid and the assistance of British troops, had been unable to prevent the insurgents from securing control over the bulk of the Greek hinterland by 1947. The British government, weary of the instability and corruption of the Greek anti-communist coalition, and faced with its own grave financial problems in early 1947, announced on 1 February that it could no longer afford to subsidise either the Greek or the Turkish armies (the Turkish army had been permanently mobilised since 1945 in the face of the Soviet threat to the Straits), and was withdrawing all support to them on 31 March 1947. The Greek insurgents were supported by Tito's Yugoslavia and by Bulgaria and, while there is evidence that Stalin did not wholeheartedly back Tito's ambitions in Greek Macedonia – he did not approve of Tito's schemes for a Balkan federation – the Americans believed Moscow would

37

welcome a communist-controlled Greece if, as seemed likely, the royalist government collapsed. While already aware of Britain's reluctance to continue propping up the Greeks, Washington was caught off balance by Britain's sudden announcement of its intention to withdraw from the Eastern Mediterranean. Nonetheless it provided Truman and his Under Secretary of State, Dean Acheson, with the opportunity to extend American protection to Greece and Turkey.

Aware of the difficulty of persuading cost-conscious Republican Senators to vote the sums necessary to succour Greece and Turkey, Truman and Acheson emphasised the communist danger, painting in lurid colours the likely spread of communist regimes in Western Europe and the Middle East if Greece and Turkey succumbed. This alarmist talk resulted in the passage of an aid bill for Greece and Turkey through Congress in May, preceded by the President's enunciation of the famous 'Truman Doctrine', promising that the United States would 'support free peoples who are resisting subjugation by armed minorities or outside pressures'. This vision of a worldwide communist conspiracy, however much it impressed American legislators, appeared to commit the United States to a universal crusade to eradicate the menace, although Acheson insisted that the United States would act only in cases where its vital interests were at stake [1: 225; 2; 4; 117].

The Greek communist insurgents were eventually defeated by the Greek army, with the help of American aid and military advisers. The United States next turned its attention to war-ravaged Western Europe. The new American Secretary of State, Marshall, returning via Western Europe to Washington from an abortive Foreign Ministers Conference in Moscow in the spring of 1947, was appalled at the economic and social distress he witnessed in Europe. The West European economies were suffering acute balance of payments difficulties caused by the need to spend scarce dollars to pay for essential imports of food and raw materials from the United States. At the same time their industrial and agricultural production languished because of a shortage of investment funds. The harsh winter of 1947 had exacerbated their difficulties by causing a severe fuel crisis and a breakdown in communications. The United Kingdom had practically exhausted the 1945 American loan, and its resumption of full sterling convertibility on 15 July 1947 led to such a drain on its meagre reserves that London was forced to suspend it on 20 August 1947.

Marshall and his advisers feared that unless generous American aid to Europe was provided soon the deterioration in the economic life of Western Europe would lead to a severe slump which would have dire effects on the American economy. An economic crisis of such magnitude might encourage the peoples of Western Europe to turn to communism and the Soviet Union for their salvation – the communist parties in France and Italy had already attracted considerable electoral support and communists occupied ministerial posts in their coalition governments.

In a speech at Harvard University on 5 June 1947 Marshall called for a determined United States effort to promote the economic revival of Europe and thus ensure the continued prosperity of the American economy. He suggested that the European governments confer about their respective financial problems and then approach the United States with a common programme, setting out the dollar aid they would require to rectify their trade imbalances with the United States, which would enable them to release funds for investment and recovery. An additional invitation was extended to the Soviet Union and the Central and East European states, although the State Department hoped that it would be refused. In view of the growing hostility in the United States towards the Soviet Union it was not very likely that Congress would have approved the vast sums the shattered Soviet economy required, or indeed would have passed the programme at all if it had been linked to massive aid to the Soviet Union. Molotov and a team of 89 Soviet economic experts turned up at the preliminary conference of the European powers in Paris on 26 June 1947, called to draw up Marshall Plan requirements, in order to discover the terms on which United States aid to the Soviet Union might be available. However, he soon abandoned the meeting, refusing to supply the economic data on which Washington insisted before credits could be extended. Czechoslovakia, which had agreed to attend a further European conference on the aid plan on 7 July 1947, was ordered by Moscow to withdraw its acceptance [4]. Stalin and Molotov could now only take refuge in the vain hope that Anglo-American differences over Germany would destroy the Marshall Plan [122].

The episode does suggest, however, that Stalin – who had assured a visiting American politician in April 1947 that he was still willing to do business with the United States – had not finally determined on a breach with the United States at this time. Yet he could not afford to open the Soviet Union to the prying eyes of Marshall Aid planners. A society which was making heavy sacrifices to rebuild Soviet industry, and which suffered a serious harvest failure in 1946, had to be sealed off from Western influences. In 1946–1947 the Soviet Communist Party launched a vicious campaign against foreign and bourgeois literature, thus reversing the relaxation in cultural controls which had taken place during the war [80].

The Western European powers drew up their Marshall Plan requirements, and after complicated negotiations they were accepted by the United States. In 1948 Truman was able to persuade Congress to provide the necessary funds under the European Recovery Act, a task assisted by a complete communist take-over of power in Czechoslovakia in February 1948, which further fuelled anti-Soviet feelings in Congress. '"We used to say," Dean Acheson wrote to Harry Truman years later, "that in a tight pinch we could always rely on some fool play of the Russians to pull us through"'[122].

The Czechoslovakian coup was the final act in the reversal of the Kremlin's policy of encouraging the formation of peoples' democracies in Eastern Europe. In 1946 and 1947 the left-wing coalitions in the region were gradually replaced by communist governments and communist collaboration with centre-left governments in Western Europe was brought to an end. With the definite emergence of two blocs in Europe, Stalin sought to bring the European communist parties, and particularly Tito's Yugoslavia which was demonstrating an unwanted independence, more firmly under Moscow's control [122]. At a meeting of the nine European communist parties in Polish Silesia from 22 to 27 September 1947 the first steps in this direction were taken by the establishment of the Communist Information Bureau, designed to provide more direct channels of communication between the Soviet and other communist parties. Zhadanov bitterly attacked Western imperialists and capitalists and called for an energetic communist propaganda campaign against warmongers. During the autumn of 1947 Western communist parties were instructed to do all in their power to bring down their governments and a wave of strikes and demonstrations against the Marshall Plan was launched. The Soviet Union hoped that this pressure upon the wavering and insecure coalition governments, particularly in France and Italy, would lead to their downfall and replacement by communist-dominated governments who would renounce both the Marshall Plan and reliance upon the United States and throw in their lot with the Soviet bloc. Thus domestic upheaval and revolution would lead to far-reaching changes in the foreign orientation of Western European countries [80].

The centre-left government of Italy managed to weather the storm, assisted by timely and much publicised injections of emergency United States aid coupled with American threats to cut off all financial assistance to Italy if the country succumbed to communism and rumours of possible American military intervention if it did so. The French government's resistance to the communist-inspired strikes and riots was also bolstered by American aid, but it was a close-run thing: many foreign observers feared that the country would become ungovernable and therefore ripe for a communist coup. The Dutch and Belgian governments had less difficulty in riding the storm. No doubt the communist-inspired violence and intimidation were in the end counter-productive, alienating the moderate elements in the West European populations which might otherwise have been more sympathetic to communist propaganda against American imperialism. They were driven into the arms of the propertied classes in defence of law and order. In the aftermath the Western communist parties and their mentor, the Soviet Union, lost a considerable amount of credibility and prestige in the eyes of former sympathisers and the uncommitted. The reputation for respectability and responsibility which they had tried to build up after 1945 was destroyed.

The Berlin Blockade and the Formation of NATO, 1948–1949

The Soviet Union also reacted angrily to developments in Western Germany where the merged British and American zones (France did not agree to merge its zone with theirs until March 1948) were moving towards the creation of an administration in which the German non-communist political parties would have a major role, with the object of formulating a federal constitution for the area. Another meeting of Western and Soviet foreign ministers in November and December 1947 produced no agreement on the future of Germany, and Stalin decided to take more direct action to force the West to reverse its German policy. Berlin had been divided into four military sectors in 1945, reflecting the zonal division of Germany, but it was supposed to be governed as an entity by the four Allied military commanders. The three Western sectors of the city were isolated deep within the Soviet zone of Germany, with long road and rail communications to the Western zones. The communications were under Soviet control and were not subject to any clear Western-Soviet agreement about access rights. Moscow's decision to cut off all road and rail traffic between West Berlin and the Western zones of Germany on 24 July 1948 was the culmination of weeks of sporadic interference with Western access to the city. The Soviet action was precipitated by the West's decision to introduce a new West German currency as the first step towards the rejuvenation of the West German economy, and a dispute with the Soviets over whether this currency should circulate in Berlin.

Larger issues were of course at stake. The Soviet Union was becoming increasingly alarmed as the West pursued the separate development of Western Germany, which pointed towards the creation of a sovereign and possibly remilitarised West German state. Soviet pressure on West Berlin was designed to persuade the West to abandon its plans for Western Germany or, if this failed, to force the West to quit Berlin while the Soviet Union built up a separate East German state tied to Moscow politically and militarily. In this situation the presence of a relatively prosperous Western bastion in the former German capital, in the heart of Eastern Germany, was an embarrassment. Furthermore, the knowledge that the West was prepared to abandon the West Berliners to their fate would cause the West Germans to pause before they associated themselves too closely with the Western powers.

Truman was determined that the West should not be driven out of Berlin by Soviet pressure. He did, however, reject a proposal by General Lucius D. Clay, the United States Military Governor of Germany, that an Allied convoy under military protection should attempt to force a passage to West Berlin. The President was anxious to avoid a confrontation which might escalate into all-out war. His advisers agreed upon a less provocative solution and from July 1948 to May 1949, when both the Berlin blockade and an Allied counter-blockade of the Soviet zone were ended, an Anglo-American airlift managed to keep the West Berliners supplied with basic fuel and food requirements. Despite a number of incidents the Soviets did not interfere with the airlift. Indeed, as a warning to the Soviet Union, Truman authorised the despatch of B-29 heavy bombers, capable of striking targets within the Soviet Union, to British bases in July 1948. Although these bombers were not modified to enable them to carry atomic bombs, Stalin's decision to call off the blockade demonstrated the failure of the Soviet Union to achieve any of its objectives. He had not called it off before in the hope that continued pressure on West Berlin might still split the three Western powers and lead them to make some concessions. He also wanted to avoid a too precipitate and humiliating Soviet climbdown. The West did, however, agree to hold another Foreign Ministers Conference in May and June 1949 to discuss the future of Germany – a meeting which was as futile as its predecessors [4; 117].

Indeed, the Berlin confrontation was, from the Soviet point of view, counter-productive. It increased Western alarm about Stalin's ultimate intentions and focused their attention more closely on the vulnerability of Western Europe to a Soviet attack. In the event of a war the United States and Britain planned to bomb Soviet cities and industries from bases in Britain and the Middle East, using both conventional and atomic weapons. However, this would not prevent the Red Army from brushing aside the weak Western European defences and occupying the area – indeed, the British and Americans planned to evacuate their occupation troops in Germany to Britain should the Soviet Union invade Western Europe. The Berlin crisis prompted the Western European states to improve their defence. In March 1948 Britain, France, the Netherlands, Belgium and Luxembourg had signed the Brussels Pact, which provided for mutual action in the event of aggression against any of the signatories. The Brussels Treaty powers promised to co-ordinate and plan their defences in advance. However, it was clear from the outset that without the material and psychological support of the United States, the relatively weak Western European states would never be able to build up their forces sufficiently to mount a credible deterrent to the Soviet Union.

The Truman administration was willing to further its increasing commitment to West European stability by contributing directly to the defence of the area. Stalin's Berlin blockade had convinced some previously sceptical Senators that the Soviet Union was a major threat to world peace, and they were now willing to jettison their isolationist sentiments and support a United States initiative in Western Europe. Supported by Republican and Democratic Senators, the Republican leader, Arthur H. Vandenberg, successfully secured the passage through the Senate of the famous 'Vandenberg Resolution' on 11 June 1948, which authorised the United States to enter into alliances with non-American powers. Negotiations were brought to a successful conclusion in April 1949 when the Brussels powers, together with the United States, Canada, Denmark, Iceland, Italy, Portugal and Norway, signed the North Atlantic Treaty, which provided for mutual defence in the case of an attack on one or more of the signatories by the Soviet Union. Greece and Turkey joined the organisation in 1952. An accompanying military aid bill provided for American military assistance to the West European armies. The ratification of this treaty by the United States still required the consent of two-thirds of the Senate and many Senators doubted that United States security required participation in such a far-reaching pact, while others were reluctant to vote for the accompanying aid bill. Dean Acheson, who replaced Marshall as Secretary of State in January 1949, persuaded many of the waverers to vote for both the Treaty and the aid bill by convincing them that the Treaty would not require the despatch of any more American troops to Europe. This promise returned to haunt the administration during the Korean War. He also insisted that the Treaty was based on the principle of mutual aid – that United States financial assistance was intended to help the Europeans to build up their own arms industries and armies and make them less dependent on the United States in the future. The Senate therefore consented to the Treaty in July 1949, but many Senators were given the impression that it was only intended to boost West European morale and encourage self-help, and thus would require few United States sacrifices beyond the initial financial outlay [62].

Cold War Developments in 1949

American satisfaction with developments in Western Europe was soon overshadowed by the startling revelation that the Soviet

Union had exploded an atomic bomb in August 1949. The loss of the United States atomic monopoly, years earlier than many of its scientists had forecast, coupled with the communist victory in China over Chiang Kai-shek's nationalist (Kuomintang) forces in the autumn, seemed alarming indications that communism was on the march everywhere. Truman had long since abandoned any hope that the corrupt and incompetent Kuomintang regime would defeat the communists in the Chinese civil war, and had no intention of committing United States troops to the nationalist side, although Chiang received United States financial aid and military equipment. Soon the legend gained ground in the Republican Party – assisted by Kuomintang propaganda in the United States – that Truman had abandoned Chiang to his fate: 400 million Chinese had been 'lost' to 'godless communism'.

The shocks inflicted on American self-confidence by these events resulted in a marked shift in the attitude of public opinion towards communism. Hitherto Americans had accepted the need to contain the Soviet Union in Europe and the Middle East fairly calmly – the situation called for firmness rather than for drastic measures and military budgets remained at a fairly low level in these years. After 1949 attention shifted to the Far East, traditionally an area of American concern, and where it now appeared that communism had achieved a major triumph. To apply the containment doctrine to this vast region was a much more complex and hazardous undertaking than in Europe: most Asian societies and governments were unstable and even turbulent, while intense nationalism might ally with, rather than against, communism in the face of 'Western imperialism', which for many was a recent and bitter memory.

The Chinese communist victory, coupled with the Soviet explosion of an atomic bomb (which demonstrated that Soviet technology was not as backward as many had assumed) had an unsettling effect on American society. 'Isolationism' in the traditional sense had all but disappeared. The United States could no longer insulate itself militarily from the rest of the world. The Atlantic and Pacific Oceans were no longer secure moats behind which the United States would have time to build up its immense potential to defeat an aggressor. Nor could the West Europeans hope to delay an invasion from the East for a sufficient period to enable the United States to complete its preparations.

However, the rise of communism in China, a country in which the United States had strong ties of sentiment resulting from intense American missionary and economic activity there, led to the formation of a powerful 'China Lobby' in the Republican Party, which called for a concentration of American resources in future on an 'Asia First' strategy, with assistance to Europe reduced to an absolute minimum. At the same time the discovery of a number of spies in the Canadian and British scientific establishments led to suspicions that the Soviet atomic bomb resulted not from its own scientific expertise but from treachery in the West. In the same way the fall of the nationalist Chinese was attributed to the activities of pro-Chinese communist traitors inside the State Department and diplomatic service. The ensuing fuss forced Truman to authorise loyalty investigations of prominent public servants – the only crime of many having been to extol the virtues of the Soviet alliance when it had been fashionable to do so during the war. This was to be the precursor of a more deadly and thorough-going anti-communist witch hunt in the 1950s.

Truman ordered the crash development of the hydrogen (H) bomb – enormously more destructive than the atomic bomb – and set up a joint State and Defence Department committee to investigate the state of United States defences in the aftermath of the explosion of the Soviet atomic device. This investigation was carried out under the auspices of the National Security Council (NSC), set up in 1947 to coordinate American defence and foreign policies. The ensuing report, filed as NSC 68, expressed in the most alarmist terms the worldwide threat posed by communism to the free world. It recommended that American military capabilities – both nuclear and conventional – be expanded so that the United States could deal with communist challenges wherever and in whatsoever form they manifested themselves. This rearmament programme should be completed by 1954 when the committee prophesied that the Soviet Union, which devoted a far larger proportion of its Gross National Product (GNP) to defence than the United States, would be fully capable of deploying nuclear weapons in a war with the West [118].

Truman wanted to keep arms expenditure as low as possible and he ignored the report. He accepted the air force view that air power, together with the vast potential power of the H-bomb, would be sufficient to deter Soviet aggression. He did authorise increased expenditure on nuclear and bomber development. Nor was he prepared to over-react to the establishment of Mao Tse-tung's communist regime in mainland China. Acheson expected that the island of Formosa (Taiwan), whither Chiang's forces had fled from the mainland after their defeat, would soon fall to the communists and he had no intention of trying to prevent a communist seizure of the island. In a speech in January 1950 Acheson stated that American security in the Pacific region depended on their bases on the island chain running from the Aleutian Islands through Okinawa and Japan to the Philippines. By implication Korea was excluded from this defence perimeter [86].

Stalin's reaction to the emergence of a new communist power in China was ambiguous. Publicly the Soviet Union welcomed the communist victory, but Stalin had done very little to help Mao's cause. When Stalin quarrelled with Tito in 1947 over Yugoslavia's scheme to set up a South Slav federation with Bulgaria, which resulted in Yugoslavia's expulsion from the Soviet bloc, he had been reluctant to unleash the Red Army against Yugoslavia which possessed an army of seasoned Second World War veterans. He had good reason to feel apprehensive about the rise of an even more independent communist state in China which might eventually rival the Soviet Union. The weak nationalist government of Chiang Kai-shek was preferable, in Soviet eyes, to a stronger communist regime. Soon Mao began to demand, and eventually achieved, the restoration of the territorial and economic concessions Stalin had wrested from the nationalists in 1945.

In 1949 a new wave of purges of both the Communist Party of the Soviet Union and those of Eastern and Central Europe showed that Stalin was determined to enforce his will inside the Soviet Union and to consolidate Moscow's control over the satellite states. Only rigid Stalinists who would not deviate from the Kremlin line remained in office. However, for the foreseeable future, Stalin could rely on Mao Tse-tung's loyalty – China was dependent on Soviet military, material and moral support, especially as the United States refused to have any dealings with the Peking regime. During a visit to Moscow in early 1950 Mao signed a treaty of mutual assistance with the Soviet Union, directed against Japan, and secured Soviet credits and material assistance [85].

The Korean War, 1950–1953

On 25 June 1950 the armed forces of the Communist ruler of North Korea, Kim Il Sung, launched a surprise attack on the Republic of (South) Korea. Korea had been liberated from the Japanese, who had annexed the country in 1910, by the Red Army in 1945. The Soviet Union and the United States had divided Korea between them for military purposes at the 38th parallel in the same year, with the Red Army occupying the north and the United States the south. Subsequent efforts to reunite the country had fallen foul of the growing antipathy between the occupying powers and, as a result, two separate regimes had developed in the country. After 1946 the Soviets sent military aid and advisers to build up Kim Il Sung's army while the United States, which had withdrawn its troops from the south in 1948–1949, provided military and economic aid to the ruler of South Korea, Syngman Rhee. When, in January 1950, Stalin was begged by Kim Il Sung to authorise an invasion of South Korea the Soviet dictator was at first reluctant to give his consent, but relented in March having convinced himself that the United States would not intervene to save Rhee's dictatorial and corrupt regime. [122] The United States did not have a formal treaty of alliance with South Korea and, moreover, Acheson had excluded the country from the United States defence perimeter in January 1950. A communist-controlled South Korea, close to the Japanese mainland, would encourage Tokyo to adopt a neutral stance in the East–West struggle. Mao, preoccupied by domestic problems and with preparing his forces for an invasion of Formosa, was in no position to oppose the invasion.

Truman ordered American air and naval forces in the vicinity to assist Rhee's forces and shortly thereafter United States army units from Japan helped the beleaguered South Koreans. In the absence of the Soviet delegate, who had boycotted the United Nations Security Council since January 1950 in protest at the non-admission of communist China to the organisation, Truman secured the passage of two United Nations resolutions at the end of June and in early July condemning North Korea for its aggression and calling on United Nations members to assist South Korea. Some of America's allies, such as Britain and France, sent token ground forces, but the bulk of the subsequent fighting was undertaken by South Korean and United States troops, under the command of General Douglas MacArthur, the commander of United States forces in the Far East.

After a dramatic United Nations landing at Inchon, on the west coast of North Korea, on 15 September 1950, the communist advance was reversed and soon the North Korean army was in full retreat across the 38th parallel. Truman authorised MacArthur to cross the parallel with the object of unifying Korea under United Nations auspices. The United Nations advance towards the Yalu River, the border between North Korea and Chinese Manchuria, led Mao to send Chinese communist troops in the guise of 'volunteers' to help the North Koreans. Despite both UN and US assurances that their forces would remain on Korean soil only until Korea had been reunified, Mao could not tolerate the presence of American troops on the frontiers of China. By December 1950–January 1951 MacArthur's forces were driven back deep into South Korea, and Britain urged the United States, faced with the possible evacuation of United Nations forces from Korea, not to widen the war by bombing China as MacArthur was demanding. London feared that such action would bring in the Soviet Union on China's side in the struggle and that the ensuing war would be worldwide. In March 1951 United Nations forces launched a counter-offensive which brought them back to the 38th parallel and bitter fighting thereafter failed to remove this frontier more than a few miles in either direction. So frustrated was MacArthur by the stalemate that in April 1951 he resumed his demand – this time publicly – for the air force to be authorised to bomb China, with nuclear weapons if necessary. Faced with this challenge, both to his authority as commander-in-chief and to his limited war strategy, Truman dismissed the general from all his commands in the Far East [59; 76; 105].

The Korean War, and particularly the United Nations invasion of North Korea, intensified the Cold War. Truman adopted the provisions of NSC 68 and ordered a major rearmament programme. Britain and France followed suit. While the Anglo-French programmes produced improved weapons and equipment for their troops, they had only a marginal effect on the defence of Western Europe. Most of France's military resources were chan-nelled into Indochina, where its generals were planning a new offensive against the communist insurgents: it had few troops left over to augment its forces in NATO. Britain too, saddled with worldwide military commitments, was equally in no position to spare additional manpower for European defence. In any case its rearmament programme was soon cut back when it resulted in increasing economic and financial difficulties. Inevitably the situation led to mounting American pressure on its allies to utilise West German manpower and industrial resources for military purposes.

Many Western defence analysts suspected that the Soviet-backed North Korean invasion of the South was a feint designed to divert American attention (and resources) from Europe, thus enabling the Soviets to force the inadequately prepared West Europeans into the Soviet bloc. While this was an exaggeration, Stalin anticipated that events in the Far East would lead to the relaxation of United States vigilance in Europe, enabling him to extract concessions in Germany or Berlin.

Inevitably the crisis in Korea strengthened the pressure of the 'China Lobby' on Truman to switch to an 'Asia First' strategy, and of course MacArthur was a leading proponent of this view. Truman believed that to adopt this strategy would result in the United States being pinned down by a secondary enemy, China, in the Far East, while the main enemy, the Soviet Union, forced its will on Western Europe. Accordingly he strengthened both theatres in 1950 and 1951. United States reinforcements were despatched to Korea while the administration decided to give Chiang Kai-shek military and financial support and moved the United States navy into the Formosa Straits to deter the Chinese communists from attacking Formosa – at the same time it prevented the nationalists from invading the mainland [59; 76; 105]. In 1951 a peace treaty was signed with Japan which tied Japan to the United States and allowed American troops to remain in Okinawa. Finally, the United States agreed to provide military assistance in 1950 to the French in Indochina. Since 1945, when their colonial possession had been restored to them, the French had been engaged in a bitter guerrilla struggle with Ho Chi Minh's communist (Vietminh) forces for control of the country. Ho was a nationalist as much as a communist, but the decision of both Moscow and Peking to recognise his movement as the legitimate government of Indochina and to provide him with aid in 1950 convinced the United States that he was an agent of the Kremlin [86].

The Recovery of West Germany

In 1951 Truman authorised the despatch of an additional four divisions of American troops to West Germany to bolster Western European defences. Many Senators were angered by this decision – they had been assured by Acheson in 1949 that the NATO treaty would not lead to a further American troop commitment to Europe. At the same time the administration began to press for the rearmament of West Germany. Since the formation of NATO the United States Department of Defense (Pentagon) had believed that the West Europeans would need to build up their forces to provide 35–40 divisions as a credible deterrent to a Soviet land invasion. However, the Europeans were unwilling to make the sacrifices necessary to achieve such a force level. Furthermore the NATO planners wanted the West European defence line moved forward from its 1950 position on the River Rhine further east to Western Germany's frontier near the Elbe, so that the resources of West Germany would remain available to the West in the event of a Soviet attack. This would also provide NATO with greater defensive depth. Given the failure of the other European powers to expand their own forces sufficiently to defend this enlarged area, Washington demanded the utilisation of West German manpower to fill the gap. This pressure was strenuously resisted by the French, fearful of the resurgence of German military power.

After the end of the war France had demanded the imposition of severe reparations burdens on Germany and had resisted Anglo-American efforts to encourage the expansion of Germany's industrial production. For the most part these French aims had been frustrated. Reparations in the Western zones had been abandoned by 1948, and coal, iron and steel production began to expand dramatically after 1949 when West Germany received Marshall Aid funds. In 1949 a West German federal government had been established and its Chancellor, Konrad Adenauer, was pressing for full sovereign rights. The French now attempted to secure West Germany's co-operation to prevent the rise of unrestrained German industrial power. In 1950 the French government put forward the Schuman Plan for a European Coal and Steel Community, to consist of France, West Germany, the Benelux countries and Italy. This French project, while establishing global production targets for these commodities, would regulate their production on a country-by-country basis. The two strongest producers (Britain refused to participate) would thereafter co-operate and not compete with each other, and the revival of the Ruhr would no longer be a threat to France.

However, the French were not prepared to agree to Germany's remilitarisation without a struggle, and certainly not on the comparatively liberal terms proposed by the United States. Since the elite of the French army was fighting in Indochina, the French could not view with equanimity the revival of German military power. They refused to yield even when Truman threatened to abandon promised American financial and military aid to NATO if France persisted with its objections.

In October 1950 the French put forward the Pleven Plan for a European Defence Community (EDC) – a scheme for a European army composed of France, West Germany, Italy, Belgium, Holland and Luxembourg, to which each member would contribute military units. This army would be under a supra-national European military organisation, with its own European Minister of Defence. As such it was designed to prevent the rise of a separate West German national army. Instead, German contingents would be closely tied to West European defence. The United States accepted this proposal in December 1950, although few military experts had much faith in the military effectiveness of such an organisation, and Britain refused to participate.

The French convened a European Army Conference on 15 February 1951 – the negotiations were to be long drawn out and contentious – and meanwhile the United States provided Western Europe with the additional troops and financial assistance it had earlier threatened to withhold. General Dwight D. Eisenhower, the wartime Supreme Commander of the Allied Expeditionary Forces in Europe, was appointed to the post of Supreme Commander of NATO on 19 December 1950 and the Supreme Headquarters of the Allied Powers in Europe (SHAPE) formally assumed its full functions at the Astoria Hotel in Paris on 2 April 1951 [44].

Conclusion

In 1945 the United States hoped to co-operate with the Soviet Union to maintain world peace and to promote world economic recovery. Similarly, Stalin had no wish to become involved in a renewed conflict, this time with the United States, and he believed that Soviet interests in the post-war world could be safeguarded by collaboration with America. President Truman did not altogether share the suspicions of Winston Churchill or some of his own advisers about the Soviet Union. Not that Churchill wanted a quarrel with the Soviet Union either: he wanted the West to adopt a policy of firmness towards the Russians which, he believed, would lead Stalin to co-operate with the West in a spirit of compromise. Subsequently Truman adopted a policy of firmness but this served merely to increase Stalin's already burgeoning suspicions of the United States.

It was the steady stream of Soviet actions in Eastern and Central Europe, in Germany, in the Eastern Mediterranean and in Iran which aroused Truman's fears about its ultimate ambitions. Individually these actions might have been passed off as Soviet efforts to safeguard its security, as in its demands for a change in the Straits regime in its favour, or its economic interests, as in the case of its pressure for oil concessions in North Iran, but collectively they appeared to the West as a deliberate programme designed to undermine Western influence in areas bordering the Soviet Union as a prelude to a complete communist take-over of these lands.

The transformation of the attitude of the United States administration and of large sections of the Senate from one of cautious optimism in the summer of 1945 about the prospects for American–Soviet co-operation, to one of implacable hostility towards Soviet designs, was not finally accomplished until 1947. However, evidence that the climate of opinion in official circles in Washington was already turning against the Soviet Union in February 1946 (and of course some officials had long-held suspicions of Soviet policy) was provided by the receptivity with which the State Department greeted the famous 'long telegram' of 8000 words sent by George F. Kennan, the United States Chargé d'Affaires in Moscow, to Byrnes on the 22nd, in answer to a query by the Secretary of State about the direction of Soviet foreign policy. This telegram was widely circulated within the Washington bureaucracy and was to provide the intellectual basis for the doctrine of 'containment' by which the United States attempted to prevent further

Soviet encroachments beyond the areas they had occupied in 1945 [64].

Kennan wrote that the combination of Russian nationalism, Marxism, the historical Russian distrust of the outside world and their sense of insecurity and inferiority *vis-à-vis* the West, made the Soviet threat to the United States a particularly dangerous one. In these circumstances there could not, in the foreseeable future, be a permanent resolution of United States differences with the Soviet Union, which would continue with its efforts both to undermine the West and to expand into regions at present outside its control. Only by a determined, patient, firm and long-term policy of resistance could the United States thwart Soviet ambitions.

This gloomy prognosis was seized on avidly in Washington both as an explanation for Soviet malevolence and as a justification for increased American vigilance. Nevertheless this official hostility towards the Soviet Union did not permeate American public opinion completely until 1947 – there still remained the possibility for a compromise between the two powers. Stalin was not anxious to risk a complete breach with the Western powers until the Marshall Plan convinced him that the United States was seeking to use its financial strength to bring Western Europe completely under its influence. The readiness of Czechoslovakia and Poland to accept American aid under the plan led Moscow to fear that the United States was also challenging Soviet control over Central and Eastern Europe [46].

The Berlin blockade in 1948 – a Soviet attempt to prevent the creation of a separate West Germany tied to the West – persuaded Truman that war might break out as a result of Soviet miscalculation of United States resolve to defend its interests in Europe. His firmness over West Berlin and United States participation in NATO in 1949 seemed to convince Moscow that Western security in Europe could not be compromised. Thereafter, until the late 1950s, the Soviet Union made no further overt moves in Europe.

The North Korean invasion of South Korea in June 1950, following Mao Tse-tung's victory in China in 1949 and the Soviet explosion of the atomic bomb in the same year, were regarded as further blows to American security. They resulted in the 'militarisation' of the Cold War. American expenditure on armaments of all kinds shot up from the comparatively low levels of the late 1940s. The armed forces of both the United States and the Soviet Union were now fully equipped for an all-out war, while the number of nuclear weapons in the arsenals of each country multiplied. The insults which each side levelled at the other in diplomatic exchanges as well as through propaganda organs were couched more in the language of adversaries at war than of peaceful members of the international community [46; 118].

The United States now found itself involved in a military conflict for the first time since 1945, and in Asia, an area where it had least expected trouble to arise. The intervention of communist China in the Korean War in November 1950 convinced Truman that the war had been engineered by Moscow as a means of distracting United States attention from Europe. American forces in both Europe and Korea were strengthened. The Cold War reached a new peak of tension in 1950 and 1951 with the United States feverishly rearming and Soviet–American relations more embittered than ever.

Truman faced considerable pressure from the pro-Chiang Kai-shek (mostly the Republican 'Asia First') lobby in the United States, and from General MacArthur in Japan, to use Chiang Kai-shek's forces and American air power to smash the communist regime in China. Truman was determined to keep the Korean War limited to the peninsula: its extension to China, he believed, would lead to Soviet intervention and nuclear holocaust. As a result, after the spring of 1951, the Korean War became stalemated along the 38th parallel. American frustration with this situation – the first war in modern American military experience where outright victory could not be achieved – boiled over into a relentless search for scapegoats, inside and outside the administration, who could be held responsible for America's successive foreign policy failures since 1949. This anticommunist crusade poisoned American politics in the late 1940s and the 1950s and made it extremely difficult for successive administrations to formulate a coherent foreign policy [104].

3 Global Stakes, 1953–1961

Eisenhower Becomes President, 1953

The victory of Dwight D. Eisenhower, Supreme Commander in Europe during the Second World War, Army Chief of Staff after 1945 and latterly Supreme Commander of NATO, in the November 1952 presidential election – the first Republican to enter the White House since Herbert Hoover in 1929 – was partly attributable to the mounting frustration of the electorate with Truman's seeming inability to end the long drawn out and inconclusive stalemate in Korea. Armistice talks between the communist and United Nations military commands had begun in the summer of 1951, but progress had been painfully slow, and in 1952 had come to an end altogether when the two sides had been unable to reach agreement on the question of the repatriation of prisoners of war. The communists insisted on their forcible repatriation, while the Americans, for humanitarian reasons and also because they sensed a propaganda victory if large numbers of communist prisoners refused to return to their homelands, demanded voluntary repatriation. Eisenhower had anchored his presidential campaign on a pledge to end the Korean War quickly if elected [76].

Recent writers on Eisenhower's presidency have tried to restore his reputation which suffered, during the 1960s, from invidious comparisons with his dynamic successor, John F. Kennedy. Eisenhower was then portrayed as an ineffectual leader who preferred golf to affairs of state, leaving much of the decision-making to his subordinates. In recent years this view has been modified significantly. The relative prosperity of the 1950s has been compared favourably with the traumas of external and internal conflict which engulfed the United States in the succeeding two decades. Eisenhower is now represented by many writers as a skilful politician who kept a firm, if discreet, control over the actions of his military and civilian advisers, who insisted on deep cuts in defence expenditures (and resisted all pressures to restore them later) and opposed costly interventions by American land forces in overseas conflicts [68]. Although the President was as suspicious of communist aims as his hard-line Secretary of State, John Foster Dulles, Eisenhower was more flexible; willing to overrule Dulles and seize opportunities to relax East–West tension, even if he remained convinced that the fundamental antagonism between the two sides was too deep to permit a genuine *rapprochement* [5; 33]. A rather more critical biographer, Piers Brendon, described Eisenhower as a true representative of the 'middle class, middle brow, middle-of-the-road Middle America' [18: 7], conservative and anti-communist, yet not fanatically so, an archetypal American of the 1950s.

During the early years of his presidency Eisenhower was inhibited from taking advantage of Soviet approaches to Washington for a relaxation of tension after Stalin's death in March 1953 by a vicious anti-communist crusade led by Senator Joseph McCarthy of Wisconsin. McCarthy began to exploit the growing fear of domestic communism in 1950 as a means of reviving his flagging political fortunes. It succeeded beyond his wildest dreams. Assisted by the spread of television across America, McCarthy soon became a national figure. For a few years, until he was finally discredited in 1954, he hounded hundreds of alleged communists in public life through the Senate Committee on Government Operations, of which he was chairman. Many of them were innocent: all their careers were destroyed. The hysteria he whipped up spread to every corner of American life – as has been shown, even the Truman administration instituted a tough 'loyalty programme' for public servants. This was stepped up by Eisenhower in 1953 when he issued an executive order authorising instant dismissal of any public official suspected of disloyalty and unreliability. McCarthy even accused former Secretary of State Dean Acheson and former Secretary of Defense George C. Marshall of being communist dupes [89]. Eisenhower, who privately abhorred him, was reluctant to speak out against him since he believed that strong action would only increase McCarthy's notoriety – 'I will not get in the gutter with that guy' – and left it to others to bring about the Senator's downfall. This eventually took place when

McCarthy turned his attention to rooting out alleged communists in the United States Army starting with an army dentist whom he accused of being a security risk. Behind the scenes Eisenhower acted against McCarthy by refusing to allow members of the executive branch to use confidential material in testimony, citing executive privilege and by releasing information that McCarthy had tried to persuade the army to give favourable treatment to his associate, G. David Schine, who had been drafted into the army in 1953. The Army–McCarthy hearings in the Senate, which were televised, began on 17 May and soon degenerated into farce, with McCarthy using vituperative language, including attacks on Eisenhower, which alienated American public opinion and moderate Republican and Democratic Senators alike. In December the Senate censored McCarthy for bringing the Senate 'into dishonour and disrepute' [5; 89].

After Stalin died on 5 March 1953, his successor, the technocrat G.M. Malenkov, sought to emphasise consumer production at the expense of both heavy industry and the Soviet armed forces. This alteration in domestic priorities would require greater contacts with the West: the Soviet Union would need access to United States technological expertise if its domestic economy was to be transformed. In his speeches, Malenkov insisted that an armed clash between communism and capitalism would be suicidal in the nuclear age. While communism would ultimately triumph, this would be accomplished by peaceful means, and meanwhile the two camps should discuss ways of reducing tension. Given the hysterical anti-communist atmosphere in the United States, Eisenhower and Dulles ignored these Soviet feelers, arguing that a real reconciliation between the two sides could only come about if the Soviet Union rejected communism and embraced true democracy.

The new Kremlin rulers did encourage Mao Tse-tung to adopt a more flexible approach to the Korean truce talks – Stalin had been the main obstacle to an armistice [122]. They wanted to end a potentially dangerous source of East–West confrontation. Mao sought to remove his forces from North Korea and concentrate on the reconstruction of China. Rumours that Eisenhower contemplated air strikes on the Chinese mainland, including the use of nuclear weapons, may also have persuaded the Chinese to give way over the prisoners-of-war question and to agree to voluntary repatriation. The Korean armistice was signed on 27

July 1953 on the basis of the division of Korea at the 38th parallel: all subsequent attempts at unification foundered on the intense suspicions between the two Koreas [76].

'The New Look' Defence Policy

The ending of the fighting in Korea enabled Eisenhower to fulfil Republican campaign promises that defence expenditure would be significantly reduced. His 'New Look' defence policy was based on increased reliance on the deterrent effect of nuclear weapons – hydrogen as well as atomic (the United States had test exploded a hydrogen bomb in November 1952) – enabling the United States to reduce the size of its conventional forces. Countries facing a communist threat would in future have to rely on their own forces for their defence, backed up by the threat of American nuclear support. In Western Europe NATO would rely more on small 'tactical nuclear weapons' and 'trip wire' conventional forces, thus saving United States manpower, although this enabled the West Europeans to go back on their earlier promises to expand their conventional forces. Britain, who was to explode its own atomic bomb, followed the American example in 1957 by announcing that it too would rely in future on its independent nuclear deterrent rather than upon large conscripted conventional forces [66; 78].

This American reliance on the threat of massive nuclear retaliation in the event of aggression was much criticised inside the United States, not only by army and navy leaders angry about ensuing reductions in manpower and ships, but also by a new group of civilian defence analysts, working in various privately funded (often by the defence industries) foundations. These critics denounced the 'New Look' as a dangerous gamble likely to force the US in the event of a crisis to choose between a humiliating climb down or the unleashing of a mutually devastating nuclear exchange with the Soviet Union. They demanded that the United States maintain sufficient conventional strength to enable it to intervene in land conflicts where the threat of nuclear war was inappropriate [88]. Neither Eisenhower nor Dulles paid much attention to these attacks on the 'New Look', believing that the fear of an American nuclear response would discourage the communists from initiating adventures such as the Korean War. Dulles felt that verbal demonstrations of anti-communist pugnacity and a willingness to go to the brink of war in the event of any communist challenge to the West would be sufficient to force the communists to back down [61]. Eisenhower had no intention of reversing his reductions in American non-nuclear military capabilities. He feared that an overemphasis on military preparedness would unbalance the American economy and ultimately menace American society and its values. He was profoundly suspicious of what he later described as 'the military-industrial complex' which, if it grew too powerful, would be able to dictate American domestic and foreign policy and turn the United States into a 'garrison state'. The United States should remain calm in the face of communist provocations and concentrate on maintaining a stable and credible defence posture [5].

Dien Bien Phu and the Geneva Conference, 1954

The first major challenge to Eisenhower's policy, and one which demonstrated his cautious attitude arose over Indochina in 1954. Despite American material assistance, which amounted to about 70 per cent of the costs of the French military effort, by 1954 the French army was losing its long struggle to subdue Ho Chi Minh's Vietminh forces. In March, when a French army corps, besieged by the Vietminh in the north-western garrison of Dien Bien Phu, faced imminent defeat, the French government appealed to the United States for military intervention as the only way of saving its army from annihilation. As a first step France requested the United States air force to bomb Vietminh positions around Dien Bien Phu. Dulles and Admiral Arthur W. Radford, the chairman of the United States Joint Chiefs of Staff, favoured the idea but the Army Chief of Staff, General Matthew Ridgway, feared that if the air strikes failed the United States would be forced to send in ground forces and that China might then intervene and the United States would be faced with another long and bloody war. Eisenhower agreed with Ridgway: moreover France had hardly helped its cause by refusing, despite American pressure, to grant real independence to its former possessions in Indochina. However, Dulles informed the French that the United States would deploy its air power if America's allies, and particularly Britain, would agree to commit forces to the fighting. Senate approval for American air action would also be essential. Eisenhower was well aware that Britain, with heavy overseas commitments and inadequate resources, would never agree to contribute troops to help the French. At the same time Congressional leaders were opposed, as the President had anticipated, to American intervention in Indochina. Eisenhower therefore refused the French request. It seems clear that the President was opposed to assisting the French in what might become a second Korean-type war. To avoid American intervention he took refuge in a typical ploy which enabled him to blame Britain and other allies of the United States for his failure to help France [5].

The French government, faced with defeat in Indochina, decided to negotiate an end to the war and, at the end of April 1954, an international conference of the powers concerned with the Far East, including communist China, opened in Geneva to discuss the future of Korea and Indochina, although no agreement could be reached on the former country which remained divided at the 38th parallel. The French army at Dien Bien Phu was forced to surrender on 7 May. This humiliation did not, however, prevent an eventual settlement of the conflict on terms which were not unfavourable to the West. The Soviet Union and communist China, anxious to end a conflict which might lead to a new East–West confrontation, pressed Ho Chi Minh to make concessions. The Vietminh and France agreed to an armistice in Indochina with a temporary partition of Vietnam along the 17th parallel. The Vietminh were to control the North and the French army the South until elections in 1956 resulted in the unification of the country, when the French would withdraw. The United States and South Vietnam refused to recognise this agreement. The United States began to supply arms and military advisers to a new South Vietnamese government controlled by an anti-communist American protégé, Ngo Dinh Diem. The French withdrew their troops in April 1956. Supported by the United States, Diem refused to agree to the holding of the all-Vietnam elections in 1956 which he suspected would result in a communist victory. Gradually the two Vietnams developed separately, with Ho Chi Minh strengthening his hold on the North and Diem, backed by the United States, consolidating his position in the South [4].

Covert Operations: Iran, 1953, Guatemala, 1954

Learning from his experience during the Second World War, Eisenhower decided to deploy covert operations as part of his Cold War strategy. In May 1951 the Iranian prime minister, Mohammed Mossadeq, nationalised assets of the British–owned Anglo-Iranian Oil Company (AIOC). The international oil companies banded together and introduced a boycott of Iranian oil. This suited American oil companies, for it ensured a healthy price for their oil. In May 1953 Mossadeq contacted Eisenhower, saying that the continuing embargo might compel him to turn to the Soviet Union for assistance. Unwilling to see Iran fall under Soviet influence, the Eisenhower administration planned to overthrow Mossadeq. In August the CIA organised street demonstrations against the regime as well as action by the army to seize control of parliament and appoint General Zahedi as premier. American-led negotiations produced an oil agreement in October 1954. It gave control of the oilfields and refineries to the Iranian National Oil Company, while a consortium of eight Western companies would purchase and distribute the oil. AIOC's stake would be 40 per cent, five American companies gained 40 per cent and 20 per cent was shared by a French and Dutch company [15; 102].

Jorge Ubico was the dictator of Guatemala from 1931 to 1944. He cultivated close ties with the country's largest landowner, the American corporation, the United Fruit Company. He also blocked any moves to organise the labour force and suppressed political debate. It is from this relationship that we derive the phrase 'banana republic'. In July 1944 Ubico was driven from power. Elections followed in December, bringing Juan Jose Arevalo to power. His six years as president witnessed political, labour and land reforms. His term of office ended in 1950 when he was succeeded by Jacob Arbenz Guzman. He continued and intensified the programme of reforms, introducing the expropriation of unused land and its re-distribution to poor peasants. In 1952 he seized 400,000 acres of United Fruit Company land. The incoming Eisenhower administration decided in 1953 that it needed to act, describing Arbenz as a communist and fostering fears that Guatemala might come under Soviet influence. While the CIA planned a coup, Arbenz, sensing an imminent assault on his position, turned to the Soviet bloc for weapons. In May 1954 a ship carrying Czech arms arrived in Guatemala, which triggered American action. In June a force led by Castillo Armas launched an attack from Honduras, supported by bombing raids from American planes. Arbenz panicked and fled the country. Armas became president, the United Fruit Company's lands were restored, and Guatemala was again a dependable supporter of the United States. Although this was seen as a great triumph for the CIA, their action only inflamed anti-American feeling in Latin America [14; 102].

The Advent of Khrushchev

In January 1955 Malenkov was ousted from the Soviet leadership by his rival, the Party Secretary Nikita Khrushchev, and by Marshal Bulganin, the former Defence Minister, who became Prime Minister. Ebullient, temperamental and outspoken, Khrushchev, allied to party hard liners like the Foreign Minister, Molotov, the Red Army generals and leaders of heavy industry, bitterly attacked Malenkov's consumerism and his willingness to treat the capitalist West as no longer a military threat to the Soviet Union. However, once in power, Khrushchev broke with his erstwhile allies and adopted many of Malenkov's policies, calling for increased production of consumer goods, the reform and expansion of agriculture, and reductions in the size of the Red Army (which fell from 5.8 million men to 3.6 million by 1960 – Stalin had increased its size in the late 1940s). He also demanded a more liberal approach to the satellite states, a Soviet reconciliation with Tito, closer relations with, and economic assistance to, Communist China, peaceful co-existence with the West and the accomplishment of communist goals by peaceful means. However he remained a '"true believer" in the mandate of the Bolshevik Revolution among the post-Stalin generation of rulers' [122].

In a major speech to a secret session of the Twentieth Party Congress in February 1956, Khrushchev denounced the evils and excesses of Stalin's rule and by implication condemned his opponents in the Communist Party, such as Molotov, who had been closely associated with Stalin during the purges. His speech, however, stopped short of a root and branch condemnation of Stalinism – Khrushchev had also been close to Stalin, and had

63

played an active role in the purges, while many of his moderate supporters in the party opposed a witch hunt against the hard liners. In May 1955 he had inaugurated a relaxation in European tension by agreeing to Allied evacuation from, and the neutrali-sation of, Austria, by withdrawing Soviet troops from occupied Finnish territory and by meeting Eisenhower and the French and British prime ministers at Geneva in July 1955 which, despite the failure of arms control proposals, led to a significant, if temporary, improvement in East–West relations.

However, Khrushchev's willingness to talk to the West contributed to the growing divergence between the Soviet Union and communist China since Stalin's death, despite Khrushchev's desire for good relations between the two countries. Mao bitterly resented Khrushchev's attacks on Stalin and the 'cult of the personality' (Stalin's) in the Soviet Union – after all the Chinese Communist Party had built up Mao as a charis-matic leader – and Khrushchev had delivered his speech without any advance consultation with Peking. Mao claimed that Khrushchev's departure from Stalinist orthodoxy would encourage separatist tendencies throughout the communist world. While Khrushchev made repeated efforts to improve relations with Peking after 1955, the divisions between them grew worse in the late 1950s. Mao feared that improved Soviet–American relations could only be achieved at the expense of Chinese interests. For his part Khrushchev was horrified by the ravages inflicted on Chinese industry by 'the Great Leap Forward' inaugurated by Mao and also by Mao's dismissal of the U.S. nuclear threat as a 'paper tiger' [122]. In 1960 Khrushchev withdrew 12,000 Soviet technical advisers from China, who were working on China's programme of modernisation. He also refused to supply China with nuclear information which had been promised earlier. Soviet nuclear scientists had visited China whose first nuclear reactor was built in 1950 with their assistance. In 1959, however, the Soviets told Mao that no further assistance on nuclear weapons would be forthcoming from Moscow. The breach became complete during the 1960s when serious border disputes arose between the two powers: China claimed large areas of the Asiatic Soviet Union as its territory and large-scale clashes resulted which could have triggered a Sino-Soviet war [75].

Khrushchev's policy led to a relaxation of the Soviet grip on the East European satellites, where many of Stalin's appointees were replaced by more moderate communists. He also embarked on an active policy of trying to wean the emerging non-communist countries of the Third World away from United States influence by offering them Soviet aid and moral support, embarking on well publicised visits to India, Burma and Afghanistan. This policy not only upset the Chinese but, when applied to the Middle East, angered London and Washington. In 1955 Czechoslovakia began to supply arms to Egypt – hitherto Britain and the United States had monopolised arms sales to the Arab States and Israel, and had attempted to maintain the military balance between them by rationing their arms deliveries. When the United States refused an Egyptian request for additional arms, Egypt turned to the Soviet bloc. While Dulles recognised the dangers implicit in Khrushchev's efforts to ally Soviet Communism with the forces of Third World nationalism, he was unable to devise a satisfactory policy to counter the threat. He failed to recognise (as indeed did the Soviet Union) that Third World nationalists would react just as sharply to Soviet interference in their internal affairs as they had to similar Western attempts.

A group of Asian and African countries, led by India, rejected alignment with either bloc, but Dulles tended to equate 'neutralism' (or 'non-alignment' as it was called) with pro-communism. His answer to communist expansionism was to complete the policy, begun by the Truman administration, of forming a network of alliances in Asia and the Middle East. After 1951 the United States entered into security pacts with the Philippines, South Korea, Formosa, Japan, Australia and New Zealand. In September 1954 it set up the South East Asia Treaty Organisation (SEATO) with France, the United Kingdom, Australia, New Zealand, Thailand, the Philippines and Pakistan, providing for joint action against aggression, and whose provisions were extended to South Vietnam. In the Middle East, the setting up, with American blessing although not with its active participation, of the Central Treaty Organisation or Baghdad Pact, consisting of Britain, Turkey, Iraq, Iran and Pakistan, increased Egyptian suspicions of British policy in the area – the governments of the member countries tended to be pro-British and anti-Egyptian [61].

The Suez Crisis 1956

Egypt had been under the control of a group of nationalist army officers led by Colonel Abdul Gamel Nasser since 1952. The British Prime Minister, Anthony Eden, believed that Nasser entertained ambitions to dominate the Middle East by destroying Britain's waning hegemony in the area. For his part Dulles was incensed by Egypt's purchase of arms from Czechoslovakia which convinced him that Egypt was moving towards the Soviet bloc. Then on 26 July 1956, following further anti-British actions by Nasser, Dulles and Eden withdrew their support for a large loan they had earlier promised Nasser to finance the construction of the Aswan Dam. In retaliation, and as a means of financing the Aswan Dam, Nasser then nationalised the British and French-owned Suez Canal Company. To Eden this was the last straw. Unless Nasser was punished his influence would triumph throughout the Middle East. While Dulles tried to seek a compromise by setting up a committee of canal users to manage the canal, the British Prime Minister entered into secret negotiations with France and Israel to find more forceful means of dealing with the Egyptian leader. France wanted to stop the flow of Egyptian arms to the Algerian nationalists, who were in open rebellion against their French rulers. Israel, facing the exclusion of its shipping from an Egyptian-owned Suez Canal, apprehensive that Nasser was seeking the leadership of the Middle East in a crusade against Israel, and angered by Egyptian-backed terrorist outrages across the Sinai desert, agreed to provide the French and British with a pretext for intervention by invading the Suez Canal. Britain and France would then call on both sides to withdraw from the Canal Zone and at the same time send an Anglo-French force to occupy the area.

In the event, however, the Anglo-French plan badly miscarried. While the Israelis launched a successful attack on Egyptian army positions on 29 October and seized the Sinai Desert, the Anglo-French forces took several days to reach Alexandria (on 4 November). The delay enabled world opinion and the United States, alike outraged by what they regarded as a flagrant act of imperialist aggression, to mobilise opposition to the Anglo-French invasion. Eisenhower, who had not been informed in advance about the invasion, had no intention of supporting this reckless act which would enable Moscow to pose as the protector of

Arab nationalism. Indeed Khrushchev proposed to send Russian 'volunteers' to help Egypt and blustered that the Soviet Union would shower Britain and France with rockets if they did not withdraw, the United States rejected a Soviet call for joint Soviet–American action against Britain and France. Instead the United States sponsored a United Nations resolution calling for the removal of Anglo-French troops and their replacement by a United Nations peace-keeping force. Britain, virtually isolated and facing American financial and oil sanctions (Nasser had blocked the Suez Canal), called off the invasion. Anglo-French troops were evacuated from Egypt on 22 December 1956. The outcome was a triumph for Nasser, despite the poor showing of his army during the invasion, and a bitter blow to British prestige. Britain's position in the Middle East never fully recovered from this debacle [4; 61]. This affair demonstrated Britain's dependence on the United States.

Ill health and the consequences of his miscalculations over Suez forced Eden to resign as Prime Minister in January 1957. He was replaced by Harold Macmillan, whose skilful diplomacy soon enabled Britain to restore close relations with the United States. This process was assisted by Nasser's failure to co-operate with the United States in the Middle East despite its support for Egypt during the Suez crisis. Indeed, Nasser's increased post-Suez prestige in the Arab world tempted him to further his ambitions in the area. Radio Cairo intensified its anti-Western propaganda throughout the Middle East. Early in 1957 an anti-Western left-wing government came to power in Syria, a result, the United States suspected, of Nasserite machinations (in January 1958 Egypt and Syria merged to form the short-lived United Arab Republic). These developments prompted Eisenhower in January 1957 to secure from Congress authority to provide economic and military assistance to any Middle East country threatened by armed aggression or internal subversion (the so-called 'Eisenhower Doctrine'). In July 1958 the pro-British King of Iraq and his Prime Minister were murdered by pro-Nasserite Iraqi army officers who thereupon withdrew Iraq from the Central Treaty Organisation. When internal unrest, which Washington claimed was inspired by Nasser's agents, spread to the Lebanon and Jordan and threatened the stability of the pro-Western governments there, Eisenhower invoked his Doctrine and sent American troops to the Lebanon.

Macmillan despatched a British force to Jordan. The regimes in these two countries survived [4].

The Hungarian Uprising, 1956

The Anglo-French invasion of the Suez Canal enabled the Soviet Union to proclaim its solidarity with the aspirations of Arab nationalism. It also distracted world attention from the Soviet invasion of Hungary in November 1956. Khrushchev's denunciation of Stalin's excesses and his support for a degree of political and economic liberalisation in the satellites had unleashed a wave of reformism in Poland and the other Central and East European countries. The ferment reached uncontrollable proportions in Hungary, where a popular revolt against its Stalinist rulers in October led to the setting up of a new government under Imry Nagy which, on 1 November 1956, announced Hungary's virtual withdrawal from the Soviet bloc.

This was too much for the Kremlin and, on 4 and 5 November 1956, Soviet troops and tanks moved into the capital, Budapest, and Nagy was deposed and arrested. He was replaced as Prime Minister by Janos Kadar, a pro-Soviet communist. American radio propaganda from Western Europe and Dulles's rhetoric about the need to 'roll back' the Soviet frontiers had deluded the Hungarians into the belief that the United States would support their revolt, but neither Eisenhower nor Dulles was willing to provoke a nuclear war by intervening in what they accepted as a Soviet sphere of influence. The result of the Hungarian uprising was a flood of Hungarian refugees to the West and frequent American-inspired United Nations resolutions calling on the Soviet Union to withdraw its forces from Hungary. Inevitably these gestures had not the slightest effect on the Soviet Union and the episode merely exposed the hollowness of 'roll-back' to any satellites who might seek to emulate the Hungarian example [85]. Khrushchev blamed Dulles's rhetoric for encouraging the uprising and began to reverse his previous relatively moderate stance. He suppressed writers and artists inside the Soviet Union and denounced Tito when the latter protested about Nagy's subsequent execution by the Soviets [122].

Indeed, the Hungarian uprising seemed to confirm Peking's criticisms of Khrushchev's policy. Dulles was not unaware of the growing rift between Peking and Moscow but he believed that, if he responded to Chinese hints that improved relations between China and the United States were possible, China would use this to play off the United States against the Soviet Union. His suspicions of Peking's ambitions were increased when in 1954 communist China declared its intention of 'liberating' nationalist-held Formosa in the near future. This was followed by heavy Chinese artillery bombardments in 1954 and early 1955 of the two nationalist-occupied islands of Quemoy and Matsu. These were repeated in 1958. Fearing an imminent Chinese invasion, Eisenhower warned China that the United States would help the nationalists to defend the islands, signed an alliance with Chiang Kai-shek late in 1954, and sent American destroyers to escort Chiang's troop reinforcements to Quemoy in the autumn of 1958. This example of American 'brinkmanship' appeared to deter China from taking any further action [5].

The Missile Gap

Khrushchev also exhibited an increasing tendency to threaten a Soviet nuclear attack on the West during periods of tension (the Suez crisis was one example of this). In 1953 the Soviet Union tested a hydrogen bomb and in August 1957 it launched an Inter-continental Ballistic Missile (ICBM) before the United States. Then on 4 October 1957, in a blaze of publicity, the Soviet Union successfully launched the world's first man-made space satellite, Sputnik I: the United States was still experimenting with a proto-type. These demonstrations of Soviet technological expertise were bitter blows to United States pride and to its confidence in its prowess in this field. There ensued inside the United States a vigorous Congressional and press campaign, supported by air force chiefs and the aerospace industry, calling for a priority American missile and space programme. Eisenhower's critics claimed that his preoccupation with defence economies had enabled the Soviet Union to overtake the United States in an area vital to its defence and security. The critics charged that the complacent and penny-pinching Eisenhower administration had allowed the Soviet Union to win a technological victory over the United States in an area in which Americans had always prided themselves on their superiority.

Democratic politicians, such as Senators John F. Kennedy of Massachusetts and Lyndon B. Johnson of Texas, seized on the issue to further their chances in the race for the Democratic presidential nomination in 1960. American service chiefs were only too willing to supply them with confidential and exaggerated information about the poor state of American defences, calculating, wrongly as it turned out, that the ensuing political pressure would force the President to increase defence expenditure.

Eisenhower refused to embark on a major arms race, although he did authorise a slight increase in missile research and development. He steadfastly rejected demands for increases in bomber production or in conventional military capabilities. Since 1956 secret flights over Soviet territory by United States U-2 photographic reconnaissance planes had provided the President with evidence which suggested that Khrushchev's claims that the Soviet Union was constructing a large number of ICBMs were fraudulent: that the Soviet Union lacked the manufacturing capacity for this. However, the sensitive nature of these surveillance operations made it impossible for the administration to refute the alarmist figures brandished by its domestic critics about the so-called missile gap: the belief that by the early 1960s the Soviet Union would have an assured superiority in nuclear weapons and delivery systems over the United States. That in fact the reverse was true was not accepted publicly by the United States government until 1961 [11; 78].

The Berlin Crisis and the Geneva Conference, 1958–1960

Khrushchev took advantage of the hysteria in the United States about the missile gap to try to achieve a diplomatic triumph over Berlin from where Stalin had failed to dislodge the West in 1948. The division of Germany into two separate republics was now virtually an accomplished fact and the problem of a West German contribution to NATO's defences had been resolved in May 1955. In August 1954 the French National Assembly had rejected the EDC. However, Anthony Eden, then British Foreign Secretary, advanced a compromise proposal in September 1954 whereby West Germany contributed armed forces to NATO through the expansion of the Brussels Pact, which was to be called the Western European Union (WEU), with the inclusion of West Germany and

70

Italy. West Germany agreed not to manufacture nuclear and chemical weapons, missiles, bombers and warships. For its part Britain agreed to maintain on a permanent basis, and as a counter to a West German army, four army divisions and a tactical air force in West Germany. This offer helped the French to accept the plan by overcoming their fear that they might be left alone to face a resurgent West Germany. In 1955 the Federal Republic of (West) Germany joined NATO and was accepted as an equal partner in Western Europe [44]. The military division of Europe was confirmed in May 1955 by the formation of a Pact of Mutual Assistance and Unified Command (the Warsaw Pact), a military alliance based on mutual defence, consisting of the Soviet Union and the Central and Eastern European States, including the (East) German Democratic Republic (GDR), but not Yugoslavia.

Khrushchev was determined to end the anomalous position of West Berlin. While the Western sectors of that city remained under Allied military control and represented an island of prosperity in the centre of the relatively impoverished East Germany, the GDR might never become a stable ally of the Soviet Union. Large numbers of professional and skilled East Germans, whose services the hard-pressed East German economy desperately needed, escaped to West Germany through Berlin. Khrushchev required a foreign policy success to strengthen his position inside the Soviet Union. In June 1957 his enemies in the party – Molotov, Lazar Kaganovitch and Malenkov – attempted to secure his dismissal at a meeting of the Party Presidium. Khrushchev outwitted them by calling for a full meeting of the Central Committee which, packed with his supporters, voted for the expulsion of Khrushchev's enemies from the Presidium. However, his opponents had been defeated but not vanquished. They remained party members and were eventually able to gain allies in the armed forces when the latter turned against Khrushchev's plan to reduce the size of Soviet ground forces and place more emphasis in the future on nuclear deterrence. Not until 1961 was Khrushchev able to manoeuvre the expulsion of the so-called 'anti-party' group (although many of them had already been exiled) from the party. Thus, even after 1957, his position remained precarious. His decision to reduce further the number of active troops in the Red Army by 1.2 million men heightened his unpopularity in military circles. Mao Tse-tung came to the aid of his enemies by condemning his revisionist policies. In retaliation Khrushchev gave no support to China during the Formosan crises and supplied India with aircraft during its border wars with China in the early 1960s [75].

In November 1958 Khrushchev announced that, unless the West agreed to negotiate the withdrawal of its troops from West Berlin within six months, the Soviet Union would sign a separate peace treaty with the GDR and turn the West's access routes to West Germany over to East German officials. This placed the West in a dilemma: they would either be forced to deal with a regime they had promised West Germany in 1955 not to recognise, or they would be faced with a new confrontation over Berlin. Eisenhower could not abandon the West Berliners in the face of Khrushchev's threats – to have done so would have demonstrated to West Germany and to America's other allies that United States protection could not be relied upon. Khrushchev calculated that the United States would not risk nuclear war over Berlin. His conviction was strengthened when the United States and Britain hinted that they might be prepared to make some concessions. However, they made it clear that these would not include the withdrawal of their troops from the city – to Khrushchev the *sine qua non* of any agreement. The most he was prepared to concede was that Berlin should become a demilitarised city under the United Nations: once this had been achieved the Western Allies would withdraw, leaving West Berlin at the mercy of the GDR. However, after the Western powers agreed to hold a Foreign Ministers Conference in July 1959 in Geneva to discuss Germany and European security problems, Khrushchev, in February 1959, postponed his six-months ultimatum. Then in a much publicised visit to the United States in September, Khrushchev mended his fences with Eisenhower, again suspended his Berlin deadline and agreed that the future of Berlin, the German question, and arms control should be discussed at a Big Four summit meeting in Paris in May 1960 [5].

Eisenhower did not believe that this summit would have any more success in resolving the German issue than previous great power meetings, but he hoped that it would at least lead to a further postponement of the Berlin issue and to a new relaxation of East–West tensions. The Americans were willing to conclude an agreement on the suspension of nuclear testing. Both the United States and the Soviet Union had recently concluded a massive series of tests and the heavy fall-out had excited widespread fears about the biological and other hazards which were being inflicted on human kind.

However, the conference collapsed almost as soon as it began: on 1 May the Soviets had shot down and captured intact a U-2 spy plane over their territory. In the ensuing fuss Eisenhower accepted full responsibility for the reconnaissance mission; he had, after all, authorised the flight. However, the President refused Khrushchev's demand for a full apology and the Soviet delegation thereupon walked out of the conference. The U-2 incident played into the hands of Khrushchev's Kremlin enemies who seized on it as evidence that the United States could not be trusted. Khrushchev cancelled an invitation to Eisenhower to visit the Soviet Union. Any hope for a recovery from the paralysis into which East–West relations had now been plunged would have to await the inauguration of a new American President in 1961 [4; 74].

Conclusion

In retrospect Eisenhower's presidency has been regarded as one of relative peace and prosperity in comparison with the experiences of his successors. In 1953 the armistice in Korea ended the hostilities there, although the division between North and South was unbridgeable. The anti-communist hysteria inside the United States subsided after 1954. Eisenhower managed to avoid active American involvement in foreign wars after 1953. His patience and firmness during periods of tension contrasted with the militancy of his Secretary of State, John Foster Dulles, who delivered frequent speeches about the evils of communism. While Eisenhower shared Dulles's intense anti-communism, he was the more flexible of the two and was not prepared to allow the Secretary of State a free hand in determining foreign policy. Dulles had been eager to send in the United States air force to assist the French at Dien Bien Phu and had been equally persistent in demanding the destruction of Chinese airfields on the mainland to forestall a Chinese assault on Quemoy and Matsu. He had also opposed Eisenhower's summit meeting with Bulganin and Khrushchev at Geneva in 1955, suspecting a Soviet manoeuvre to trick the West into lowering its guard. Eisenhower overruled his Secretary of State in all these cases – the United States did not assist the

French by actively intervening in Indochina in 1954; the Quemoy and Matsu crises did not lead to war with China; and the President insisted on attending the Big Four Conference in Geneva in 1955, although the practical results were minimal [61].

Nevertheless the anti-communist climate in the administration and in Congress did inhibit Eisenhower from embarking on a far-reaching exploration of the possibility of reducing American–Soviet tension after Stalin's death. In any case he shared many of their assumptions about the evils of communism. His dealings with the Soviet Union were dilatory and essentially negative. At Geneva the President put forward a dramatic proposal for the United States and the Soviet Union to open up each other's air space to aerial photography by each side – the so-called 'Open Skies' initiative. In Eisenhower's view this would be a confidence-building measure, looking forward to more concrete negotiations about arms control. When Khrushchev rejected the suggestion as a blatant American effort to engage in espionage operations over Soviet territory, Eisenhower dropped the matter and made no further suggestions. Even if the Paris summit of 1960 had not collapsed over the U-2 incident, it is doubtful whether it would have accomplished much in the area of arms control. The two superpowers had been discussing a possible test ban treaty in reaction to increasing international alarm about the dangers of nuclear fall-out from the stream of tests that were carried out in these years. While both the United States and the Soviet Union did eventually stop testing on a voluntary and temporary basis, there could be no permanent ban during a period of rapid technological change and experimentation, and while each side was competing with the other in missile development [32].

Despite Dulles's pre-election rhetoric in 1952, the nature of containment did not change much between 1949 and 1960. Eisenhower followed Truman in trying to apply the concept to Asia – an almost insuperable task given the political instability and intense nationalism which characterised the area. Acheson had applied the metaphor of a rotten apple in a barrel of apples which was likely to affect the rest in trying to convince Congress of the need to assist Greece and Turkey in 1947: on this analogy, if the two countries fell to communism, the rest of Europe and the Middle East would eventually follow [1]. Eisenhower followed Acheson's example on 7 April 1954 in discussing the dangers of Indochina falling to communism, although he applied the 'falling domino' analogy: 'You have a row of dominoes set up, you knock out the first one, and what will happen to the last one is the certainty that it will go over very quickly.' Thus, if Indochina became communist-dominated, the contagion would spread to the rest of Asia [5: 180].

Eisenhower's decision to provide military and financial aid to Diem's Republic of (South) Vietnam and to build up that country as an anti-communist bastion in Indochina was to involve his successors in an expanding and dangerous commitment. His support for, and encouragement of, the subversion of allegedly anti-American regimes in the Middle East and Latin America by the Central Intelligence Agency (CIA), a policy espoused even more enthusiastically by subsequent incumbents of the White House, was to have unpleasant repercussions on America's international reputation and on its internal constitutional processes when it was revealed later. The plan to use Cuban refugees to invade Cuba and overthrow the Castro regime was approved by Eisenhower. Yet, despite all this, Eisenhower's presidency saw communism firmly established in North Korea, North Vietnam and Cuba [18].

By 1960 there was a rising tide of dissatisfaction within the United States about the lacklustre performance of the Eisenhower presidency. The support which the President had so long enjoyed in Middle America fell away after 1957 as his adminis-tration became associated in the public mind with economic stagnation and defence and foreign policy failures. His increasing ill health also told against him. All this was bound to have an adverse effect on the election prospects of Richard M. Nixon, his Vice-President, who was selected as the Republican presidential candidate in 1960. By contrast, John F. Kennedy, the Democratic presidential candidate, was to appeal to many Americans as a man who would revive America's prestige in the world after the setbacks the United States had suffered during the Eisenhower years. Kennedy promised to revitalise the flagging American economy, devote more resources to defence expenditure, reinvig-orate America's demoralised allies and embark on an active policy of countering communism in the Third World by a vigorous assertion of American values and by liberal, yet responsible, injections of American aid [7; 33; 90].

4 From Crisis to Détente, 1961–1968

Kennedy Becomes President

As Democratic candidate for the presidency in 1960 Kennedy had campaigned vigorously on the issue of American defence unpreparedness and on the dangers of the 'missile gap'. He had distanced himself from Eisenhower by stressing his youth and vigour (he was 43 in 1960: Eisenhower was nearly 70). He contrasted his bold programmes for a reinvigorated United States ('getting the United States moving again') with Eisenhower's feeble and lacklustre policies. Domestically this meant economic expansion and full employment, while in foreign policy terms his 'New Frontier' rhetoric insisted that in future the United States would ally itself with the progressive forces in the world. Nationalism would no longer, as in Dulles's day, be regarded as a potential threat to the free world – indeed, the United States would encourage and assist Third World aspirations. In his inaugural speech the new president declared that 'we shall pay any price, bear any burden, meet any hardship, support any friend, oppose any foe to assure the survival and success of liberty' [46: 205]. This high-flown language presaged a more active policy, as universalist and anti-communist as Eisenhower's had been, but under Kennedy and Johnson, armed with sufficient military strength to enable the United States to act more decisively in situations where Eisenhower would probably have been more cautious [46].

Under Kennedy and his Defense Secretary, Robert McNamara, a statistical wizard who had been president of the Ford Motor Company, defence expenditure on both nuclear and conventional forces was dramatically increased. McNamara sought to rationalise and reform the American defence establishment and bring it more closely under the control of the Defense Department. The Democrats argued that an expanding American economy could afford to devote more resources to defence. Tight budget ceilings would be lifted although McNamara insisted that, by applying cost-benefit analysis methods, he would ensure that cost overruns on defence projects, the needless duplication of weapons systems and waste in the armed forces would be eliminated. The ensuing detailed and centralised scrutiny of all weapons procurement and development processes by civilian analysts based in McNamara's office angered the United States military chiefs, who complained that the system undermined their professional expertise and led to civilian interference in operational matters.

Nevertheless the Joint Chiefs of Staff welcomed the expansion of their defence budgets which enabled them to increase the size of the United States army and navy. Expenditure on land- and sea-launched Intercontinental Ballistic Missiles (ICBMs) was also increased, but Kennedy soon discovered that the missile gap was a myth: not only did the United States have a superiority over the Soviet Union, but the Eisenhower administration had also developed more advanced solid-fuel-fired types which were quicker to fire and more accurate. This enabled McNamara to phase out some of the older first-generation liquid-fuelled missiles and to concentrate on the solid-fuelled Minuteman I and II ICBMs in hardened (heavily protected) silos and on the development of the relatively invulnerable Polaris submarine-launched missiles. By 1962 the United States possessed 250 land-based ICBMs, 144 Polaris missiles on 9 submarines and 630 B52 bombers. The Soviet Union had only 75 land-based ICBMs and 120 long-range bombers [11].

Kennedy had been privately informed by the Eisenhower administration during the 1960 election campaign that the missile gap did not exist, but continued to denounce the inadequate defence preparations of the Republicans: after all, the continuation of the missile gap myth was a strong card in his appeal to the voters and the fabrication fitted in with the perceptions of many Democratic voters about the feebleness of the previous administration. However, the knowledge of American missile superiority gave Kennedy greater confidence in dealing with Khrushchev's threats to sign a separate peace treaty with East Germany and was crucial to Kennedy's success in confronting the Soviet Union during the Cuban missile crisis in 1962.

The Bay of Pigs Invasion

Kennedy's first venture into the military arena in 1961 was a disaster. In 1959 a Cuban nationalist, Fidel Castro, with a few supporters, had overthrown the dictator, Fulgencio Batista, in Cuba. Liberal Americans at first welcomed Castro, believing that he would establish a Western-style democracy in Cuba. They soon became disillusioned, however, when Castro set up a one-party state in close collaboration with the communists and began to encourage the spread of revolution elsewhere in Latin America. Business interests were also angered when he began to nationalise United States companies in Cuba. The United States retaliated by imposing economic and financial sanctions on Cuba and breaking off relations. Castro then turned to the Soviet Union for financial and military assistance. The CIA, established in 1947 under the National Security Act to co-ordinate and collect information about potential enemies of the United States, had engaged in numerous covert activities overseas in the 1950s, including the overthrow of the anti-Western nationalist Prime Minister of Iran, Dr Mossadeq, in 1953, and a coup which had overthrown President Arbenz of Guatemala in 1954. The CIA was already planning numerous measures to overthrow or assassinate Castro when Kennedy entered the White House in January 1961. One of the most promising of these was the arming and training of anti-Castro Cuban refugees in Florida in preparation for an invasion of Cuba. Kennedy, new to the presidency, and assured that the mission would be successful, authorised the invasion, although he insisted that there should be no direct involvement of American regular forces. The invasion was a fiasco: after landing on the Bay of Pigs in Cuba on 14–15 April the American-backed anti-Castro forces were soon either killed or rounded up by Castro's troops. Kennedy's veto had prevented American air strikes which might have turned the tide in favour of the invaders. This was a major setback for Kennedy's prestige and may well have convinced Khrushchev that the youthful president was a bungling amateur [4].

The Vienna Meeting, June 1961

On 2 and 4 June 1961 Kennedy met Khrushchev in Vienna. The meeting was not a success: Khrushchev threatened Kennedy with a new six-months ultimatum for ending the unsatisfactory status of West Berlin, and warned the new president that the USSR would continue supporting anti-Western guerrillas in the Third World. The only positive result of the meeting was an agreement on the establishment of a neutralist government in Laos, a country torn by civil war between American-supported right-wing forces and a communist-supported insurgent movement, the Pathet Lao. Neither the Soviet Union nor the United States was anxious for a major confrontation in Laos, a state crucial to the interests of neither. East–West tensions remained acute after the Vienna meeting as Khrushchev continued to threaten that he would turn the Berlin access routes over to the East Germans, and Kennedy insisted that the West would never abandon its rights in the city. In July 1961 Kennedy recalled the United States reserve forces to active duty and announced a 25 per cent increase in US military strength as a clear warning to the Soviet Union not to push the Berlin question too far. For the time being Khrushchev stayed his hand.

Vietnam

On assuming the presidency, Kennedy inherited problems in South-East Asia. The Geneva Conference of 1954 had replaced French Indochina with three states. Cambodia was reasonably prosperous and stable under the authoritarian rule of Prince Sihanouk. Laos, however, was less stable and, unlike Cambodia, failed to prevent foreign intervention. By the late 1950s there was a civil war between the royal government and the Soviet-aided Pathet Lao, aided by the Soviet Union, but it did not escalate. Agreement at the Vienna summit led to negotiations which produced, in June 1962, a scheme for a neutral government in Laos. Although the civil war later resumed, and caused the Kennedy administration a good deal of concern, it did not prove a major focus of US-Soviet tension.

The deteriorating situation in South Vietnam was less easily resolved. The new president continued Eisenhower's policy of supporting the Diem regime with military and financial assistance. However, after 1960 increasing communist guerrilla (Viet Cong) activity in the south, backed by Ho Chi Minh in Northern Vietnam, led to the progressive demoralisation of the South Vietnamese army, and forced Kennedy to expand the numbers in the US military mission in South Vietnam from 685 in 1961 to 16,732 in 1963 [43: xii] and to authorise them to fight alongside the South Vietnamese army in the field. When Diem's autocratic rule provoked highly publicised acts of civil disorder among South Vietnam's Buddhist community, and rumours reached Washington that Diem was contemplating peace negotiations with the North, a CIA-backed South Vietnamese army coup against Diem took place on 1–2 November 1962. Kennedy neither authorised nor vetoed the plan. Diem and his brother were assassinated. This resulted only in increasing political instability in Saigon as contending military factions struggled for power. Kennedy fully accepted Eisenhower's assumption that the independence of South Vietnam was vital to United States security in South East Asia. He shared the previous administration's belief that if Saigon fell to Ho Chi Minh's Viet Cong, the United States would not only have sustained a major defeat in the struggle with world communism but other countries in the area would lose faith in America's ability to defend them and would speedily succumb to communism. As a result the United States would face a communist-dominated Asia, and the virus might spread to Japan, which would be cut off from its markets and sources of food. Besides the global struggle against communism and the need to establish American credibility with allies and foes alike, the administration was influenced by local circumstances. If Laos was a small country, Vietnam had a population of 14 million. It had the potential to be a major supplier of rice. Moreover, being a coastal state, it could be more easily supplied with US military and economic aid than could land-locked Laos. In addition, there was the need to reassure the Japanese and South Koreans, in order to encourage their burgeoning economies. Kennedy also suggested another influence on his policy towards Vietnam: 'I can't give up a piece of territory like that to the communists, and get the American people to reelect me' [81: 101–102]. However, he refused the advice of his military and civilian advisers that the United States should commit US regular forces to the support of the South Vietnamese army, which was sustaining defeat after defeat at the hands of the Viet Cong. Nor would he agree to air strikes by the United States air force against North Vietnam. He feared that these steps would mark the beginning of a major United States military commitment to what might turn out to be a long drawn out and bloody struggle. The problem of Vietnam was a legacy Kennedy left to his successor, Lyndon B. Johnson [4; 51; 104].

The Cold War Comes to Africa

The Congo crisis saw Khrushchev's first major foray into Africa. Neither the Soviet Union nor the United States had any substantial economic interest in the country. On 30 June 1960 Belgium, faced with growing nationalist pressures, abruptly gave independence to its colony. Almost immediately afterwards the Congolese army mutinied over the continued presence of white Belgians in its senior posts. The Belgians had done little to prepare the Congo for independence – trained Congolese personnel were virtually non-existent. Belgium rushed in troops to protect their nationals. At the end of 1960 four regimes had emerged in the Congo. The first, Katanga with its valuable copper mines, declared its independence on 11 July under Moshe Tshombe, and was defended by the recently arrived Belgian army and supported by Western mining companies. The second was diamond-rich South Kasai which had also broken away in the aftermath of the Congolese army revolt. There were also two competing regimes, both claiming to be the legitimate successors to the Belgians, under rival leaders Joseph Kasavubu in Leopoldville, who had been appointed the first president of the Congo, and the radical nationalist, Patrice Lumumba, in Stanleyville, the first prime minister. Since the latter two loathed each other, there could be no co-operation between them. Lumumba sought Soviet military assistance to oust Belgian forces from the Congo (he had first requested American help but Dulles had refused, accusing Lumumba of being a communist stooge).

The growing crisis and the fear of a major Cold War conflict in the Congo led the United Nations Secretary General,

Dag Hammarskjöld, to obtain United Nations authorisation for the despatch of a UN peacekeeping force to restore order and secure the removal of the Belgian troops, but it lacked a mandate to reintegrate Katanga with the Congo. To prevent Soviet intervention Hammarskjöld ordered the closure of all Congolese airports to all powers except the United Nations, thus Soviet planes could not be used to assist Lumumba. This move infuriated Khrushchev who accused the UN of supporting Western interests in the Congo and began an unsuccessful campaign to have three Secretary Generals of the United Nations – one from the West, the second from the Soviet bloc and the third from the non-aligned nations. Lumumba, deprived of Soviet assistance, also turned on the UN but Kasavubu, with United States support, dismissed Lumumba from office on 5 September 1960, and replaced him by Colonel (later General) Joseph Mobutu who then proceeded to imprison Lumumba (he soon escaped) and dismiss the Congolese parliament. The CIA helped in the murder of Lumumba in Katanga in January 1961, but this did not lead to a solution of the crisis.

The Kennedy administration, alive to the increasing significance of Africa in the developing Cold War situation in the continent, adopted a more pro-African policy than Eisenhower would ever have considered. While Mobutu claimed to be the legitimate ruler of the Congo a new rival had emerged in Stanleyville, a former Lumumba supporter, François Gizenga, who claimed that he had inherited Lumumba's mantle as prime minister of the country. Katanga continued to remain a secessionist entity. Hammarskjöld was now determined to use military pressure to get rid of Tshombe and reintegrate Katanga into the Congo. This policy was supported by Afro-Asian opinion which regarded Katanga as a creation of Western imperialism. In this he was also supported by the Kennedy administration but bitterly opposed by Belgian and other Western mining interests which feared that if Gizenga prevailed their financial interests in Katanga would be threatened, and the Soviets would be provided with further opportunities to meddle in Congolese affairs. Britain feared that Roy Welensky's Central African Federation, which had been providing Tshombe with arms, would be embroiled in any conflict which broke out over Katanga. Hammarskjöld was killed in an air crash en route to meet Tshombe in Northern Rhodesia in September 1961. Eisenhower had opposed Hammarskjöld's initiative as likely to encourage renewed Soviet intervention in the country. President Kennedy, however, brushed aside British and European objections and backed a UN effort to end Katangan independence. Not until January 1963 were the Katangan secessionists, who had been bolstered by white mercenaries, defeated (Tshombe fled the territory in December 1962) and Katanga reabsorbed into the Congo. A new prime minister, Cyrille Adoula, failed to cope with the continuing instability in the country as Lumumbist rebels, supported by the Soviet Union, took up arms against the Adoula government and seized large numbers of mainly Belgian hostages. Belgian paratroopers were flown in to the Congo in American planes to crush this revolt. Now the Congolese army, which had been reorganised with American help, and led by Mobuto, put down fresh rebellions. Mobutu seized power in January 1965. His repressive dictatorial regime over the Congo – which he renamed Zaire – lasted until 1997 [24].

The Cuban Missile Crisis

In the autumn and winter of 1962 Kennedy was facing a much more serious crisis nearer home. The Soviet Union had begun supplying Castro with military equipment and advisers in 1962, but stressed that this was a defensive measure. On 14 October 1962, however, American aerial reconnaissance over Cuba detected the presence of a launching pad and medium-range ballistic missiles, supervised by Soviet technicians. There is little doubt that this dangerous manoeuvre was Khrushchev's effort to secure the foreign policy success which had so far eluded him over Berlin, where Western determination to uphold the *status quo* had forced the Soviet leader to lift another six-months ultimatum he had issued to Kennedy in Vienna. He was facing continued opposition to his internal policy from the remaining hardliners in the party, who were now joined by Red Army chiefs, who forced him to cancel the troop reductions he had announced in 1960 and to increase the Soviet military budget by one-third. A dramatic overseas success against the United States would enable Khrushchev to confront both his internal critics and Beijing, and rally the moderate forces in the party to resume the task of reform and *détente*.

The Kennedy administration had made it clear in September 1961 that it possessed a two-to-one superiority over the Soviet Union in ICBMs. The positioning of Soviet Medium Range Ballistic Missiles (MRBMs) in Cuba, capable of striking at targets inside the United States, would to some extent redress the nuclear balance in favour of the Soviet Union. Khrushchev was due to visit the United Nations General Assembly in New York in November 1962 and no doubt he intended to announce his Cuban missile coup in dramatic terms there as a prelude to demanding the withdrawal of Allied troops from Berlin. It was a typical Khrushchev move – an impulsive and risky action designed to take his enemies by surprise but one which could be justified by reference to the stationing of American MRBMs in Italy and Turkey, and by the need to defend Cuba against further American-supported invasions. Future arms limitation talks would also prove more meaningful if the USSR was in a position of near equality in missiles with the USA [107].

Khrushchev completely underestimated Kennedy's combative psychology. The president was bound to react vigorously, especially with mid-term Congressional elections due in November 1962. United States indignation was increased by repeated Soviet assurances to American diplomats that it would not place offensive weapons in Cuba. At the end of October Kennedy held frequent and exhausting meetings with his closest political and military advisers – McNamara, Dean Rusk (the Secretary of State), the Joint Chiefs of Staff, his brother (Attorney General Robert Kennedy) and White House aides – to work out a response to the Soviet move. This committee, the Executive Committee of the National Security Council (ExComm), considered a number of possibilities: to do nothing, which would be unthinkable both for political and diplomatic reasons; to use American troops to invade the island and destroy the missile sites, which would risk a nuclear confrontation with the Soviet Union; or to try to destroy the sites by surgical air attacks, which might equally result in such a confrontation, as Soviet technicians would be killed. The arguments ranged to and fro between the various options. Eventually Kennedy decided to adopt a more gradual, controlled response which would enable Khrushchev to back down without being totally humiliated.

In a television broadcast on 22 October Kennedy revealed to the American people the Soviet activities in Cuba, and warned

84

the Soviet Union that 'any missile launched from Cuba against any nation in the Western hemisphere [would be regarded] as an attack by the Soviet Union on the United States requiring a full retaliatory response upon the Soviet Union' [74: 228]. He announced that Cuba would be 'quarantined' by the United States navy: all vessels bound for the island would be stopped and searched and any found carrying missiles would be turned back. United States marines were massed in Florida, while Soviet diplomats in Washington were left in no doubt of Kennedy's determination to secure the removal of the missiles from Cuba. During the ensuing few days tension mounted as Moscow protested about the blockade and stated that, in accordance with international law, Soviet vessels would refuse to allow themselves to be searched. However, on Friday 26 October Khrushchev backed down. In a long and rambling letter to Kennedy he promised that the missile sites in Cuba would be closed down and the MRBMs returned to the Soviet Union if the USA would end the blockade and promise not to invade Cuba. Later that night, however, a second note arrived in Washington which adopted a more truculent tone, demanding that in return for the removal of Soviet missiles from Cuba, the United States should remove its missiles from Turkey. This note was no doubt inspired by Khrushchev's conservative critics in the Kremlin, who had from the outset entertained serious reservations about his Cuban escapade, and who now demanded that he should at least obtain some *quid pro quo* from the United States in order to salvage something from the wreckage. Kennedy, who refused to give any such undertaking (although he later ordered the removal of the obsolescent US missiles from Turkey), decided to ignore the contents of the second note. On 27 October, on instructions from Moscow, all Soviet ships carrying MRBM equipment for Cuba were turned back and the MRBM sites in Cuba were dismantled. The United States had won a decisive diplomatic triumph. The Berlin issue also died down as a major problem in East–West relations. The East Germans had erected a wall between East and West Berlin in August 1961 and this had effectively brought to an end the flow of refugees from the GDR to the West. The GDR now achieved a form of stability it had hitherto lacked [4; 65].

In retrospect the Cuban missile crisis led to the changed atmosphere in Soviet–American relations in 1963. Both sides had been shaken by the nearness of their approach to nuclear war in 1962. Khrushchev was now anxious for an improvement in relations with the United States. He was faced with a rising tide of criticism from within the Soviet hierarchy about his clumsy diplomacy which had resulted in a resounding blow to Soviet pride and prestige. Beijing bitterly attacked his Cuban climb-down. Everything conspired against Khrushchev: even his bid for agricultural expansion in the Soviet Union resulted in spectacular harvest failures in 1963 [75].

In the United States the influence of high-level Pentagon and State Department officials, the service chiefs and key Cabinet ministers on decision-making during the crisis was significant, although Kennedy had of course the final word. Truman and Eisenhower had kept the civilian and military bureaucracy at a distance and had tended to consult their subordinates only after they had made up their own minds about policy. Kennedy appeared to be more willing to listen to his officials' advice before making a decision. Moreover, while Eisenhower had been scrupulous in keeping Congressional leaders informed about developments, for instance during the crisis over Dien Bien Phu, Kennedy imparted only general information irregularly. Admittedly events during the Cuban crisis moved too fast to permit of close and frequent consultation between the president and Congress, but nevertheless their role was relatively insignificant. If major hostilities had ensued there would have been no time for Congress to debate a declaration of war on the Soviet Union. Throughout, Kennedy relied on his power as Commander-in-Chief to determine military policy, a power which was to be employed more frequently by his successors.

US-Soviet Relations After the Cuban Missile Crisis

The Cuban missile crisis had a number of significant consequences for US-Soviet relations. In the first place, it made both governments anxious to avoid misunderstandings which, in a nuclear age, could have such frightening results. They were more willing to pursue co-operation. They were keen to improve communications, which had proceeded so slowly during the Cuban missile crisis that Khrushchev 'was using American journalists and even Radio

Moscow to relay his proposals' [96: 180]. In June 1963 a radio telephone 'hotline' was installed between the Kremlin and the White House to facilitate immediate and direct consultations between the two leaders in the event of a crisis. Also in June President Kennedy gave a speech at American University suggesting that the two countries attend to their 'common interests and to the means by which differences can be resolved' [81: 97]. 'We must deal with the world as it is'. Yet there was some ambiguity in JFK's position. In that same month he took a tougher line during a visit to Berlin. Meanwhile, there was progress on a nuclear test ban. The collapse of the Paris summit in 1960 had put an end to discussions about a nuclear test ban treaty, although both the United States and the Soviet Union had ended testing for the time being. In September 1961, however, the Soviet Union resumed testing and the United States followed suit. The preliminary round of talks on the test ban question in the late 1950s had in any case been deadlocked by arguments about underground testing. Atmospheric testing could be detected easily by seismographic means, but not so underground tests, which could be confused with subterranean earthquakes. The United States had therefore insisted that an international inspectorate should be formed to monitor underground tests on site: the Soviet Union, which had always resisted what it regarded as a form of spying, at first demurred, although it later agreed to a limited number of inspections on its soil, but these were regarded as inadequate by the American side [32]. After the Cuban missile crisis, talks were resumed in Moscow between the United States, Britain and the Soviet Union in July 1963. In August they signed a Limited Test Ban Treaty (France refused to join them) that banned testing in the atmosphere and under water; any future test must take place underground. By the late 1960s 100 nations had agreed to adhere to it. In October 1963 America supported a UN resolution banning nuclear weapons in space. The Soviet Union abandoned its opposition to spy satellites because it now had its own with the Kosmos programme.

A second consequence of the October crisis was the Soviet decision to seek nuclear parity with the United States. Americans had felt confident of their ability to compel the Soviets to back down over Cuba because of their overwhelming nuclear superiority. This led the Soviet Deputy Foreign Minister, Vassily Kuznetsov to declare: 'You will never be able to do this again' [81: 94, 96]. The Soviet Union embarked on a nuclear arms buildup. By the mid-1960s, then, both superpowers could inflict horrific damage to their adversary in any war. This gave rise to the concept of Mutual Assured Destruction (MAD). Allied nuclear strategy had evolved from massive retaliation in the 1950s to 'flexible response' in the 1960s. Instead of threatening a nuclear strike against the Soviet Union, should they attack any NATO territory, the policy would be to respond in kind. So, for example, an invasion of West Germany would produce a response from NATO's conventional forces. Nuclear proliferation – France in February 1960 and China in October 1964 exploded their first atomic bombs – also inclined the two superpowers to consider détente. So too did the financial costs of their arms race. Nuclear parity provided a vital precondition for any possible pursuit of détente.

New Leaders: Lyndon Johnson, Brezhnev and Kosygin

These developments unfolded under new leaders in both superpowers. In November 1963 President Kennedy was assassinated and replaced by Vice-President Lyndon B. Johnson, who went on to win the 1964 presidential election in a landslide. LBJ was a crude but shrewd Texan politician of considerable experience. He was assiduous in recording whom he owed and who owed him and was shameless in using the legislative pork barrel. He deployed the treatment, a skilful blend of country boy flattery, more forceful cajolery and outright bullying. His interests lay in domestic social reforms and he had only a limited knowledge of foreign affairs. He was a committed supporter of Franklin Roosevelt's New Deal. He managed in his first year as president to pass an impressive range of social legislation, unrivalled since the days of FDR [27; 28]. After the missile crisis there was a struggle for power in the Kremlin. In October 1964 Khrushchev was replaced by the joint leadership of Leonid Brezhnev as General Secretary of the Communist Party (a post known as First Secretary, 1953–1966) and Alexei Kosygin as Chairman of the Council of Ministers. An emergency Central Committee plenum on 14 October 1964 decreed that no one individual could hold both posts simultaneously. Brezhnev 'was a machine politician, a glad-handing bully with large and self-indulgent appetites, who also shared Johnson's passion for driving large American cars very fast' [110: 190]. Like Johnson he was adept at manipulating the party organisation. He had learned to avoid developing independent opinions, adjusting, instead, to the shifts in official policy. In his efforts to stabilise politics and administration after the turbulence of Khrushchev, Brezhnev restricted cultural freedom. But in the face of dissident activities, he and his colleagues did not deploy violence. Kosygin was a technocrat, interested in pursuing efficiency and economic reforms within the existing system. He was progressively outmanoeuvred by the underrated Brezhnev, who emerged in the 1970s as the dominant figure in the Kremlin.

De Gaulle

Besides its effects on the superpowers, the Cuban missile crisis also had an impact on Western Europe, and France and West Germany in particular. Both states concluded that the Americans would pursue their own interests even when their policy might risk European lives. President de Gaulle, French president since 1958, spoke of 'annihilation without representation' [81: 97]. So, while tension between the Soviet Union and the United States receded in 1963, the United States was facing increasingly difficult relations with its main European ally, France. As early as 1956, France's relations with the United States began to deteriorate: France deeply resented the American economic and financial pressure which had caused Britain to withdraw so precipitately from the Suez imbroglio, dragging France with it. After its withdrawal from Indochina, France found itself faced with new upheavals in Algeria, where fighting had broken out between Algerian nationalists, who sought independence, and the French army. France had granted its other possessions in North Africa – Morocco and Tunisia – independence in 1955. It was determined, however, not to yield Algeria, which it regarded as part of France, and which contained a large number of French settlers, or *colons*, who were vociferous in their insistence that Algeria remain French.

American pressure on France to grant Algeria independence was bitterly resented in Paris and by the *colons*, while even more provoking to French pride were speeches by United States Senators, including John F. Kennedy, condemning French army excesses in Algeria. By 1958 the Fourth Republic faced civil war as the *colons*, aided by sections of the French army, threatened to take over the central government. General Charles de Gaulle returned to power in France, dealt decisively with the insurrection-ists, and gradually withdrew the French army from Algeria, which became independent in 1961. De Gaulle had meanwhile established the Fifth Republic which, for the first time since 1851, gave the presidency, which de Gaulle occupied, considerable powers over internal and external policy.

De Gaulle was determined to restore France's global standing; to assert his country's independence from the Anglo-Saxons (US and Britain); and, not least, to secure his status as an international statesman. In 1961 France tested an atomic bomb, the basis for its independent deterrent, the *force de frappe*. De Gaulle had already, in 1958, challenged American domination of NATO, demanding that the United States, France and Britain set up a three-power directorate to run the organisation – a demand rejected by the United States as likely to alienate the other members of NATO. De Gaulle also doubted that the United States would risk its own destruction by employing its nuclear arsenal in the event of a Soviet attack on Europe. Periodic debates in Congress over the need to retain expensive United States ground troops in Germany increased French doubts about American reliability. De Gaulle called for genuine sharing of nuclear decision-making between Britain, France and the United States instead of American monopolisation of that weapon; a demand Washington also rejected [54].

De Gaulle bitterly attacked Britain's role in Europe. After Suez Britain seemed to the French to be drifting more and more into the role of a Washington satellite, suspicions which were increased by the close nuclear relationship between Britain and the United States. During the late 1950s Britain had embarked on the devel-opment of its own intermediate ballistic missile, Blue Streak, but in 1960 it had abandoned it in favour of purchasing a more advanced American model, Skybolt. This would, it hoped, enable it to keep her ageing fleet of long-range V-bombers operational down to 1970. In 1962, as part of his standardisation programme, McNamara had cancelled the production of Skybolt in favour of developing the more effective and more easily concealed submarine-launched missile, the Polaris. Anxious to end nuclear proliferations which would complicate future arms limitation negotiations, McNamara was at first unwilling to provide Britain with a replacement for Skybolt, but then Macmillan appealed to Kennedy on the issue. At a meeting with the British Prime Minister at Nassau in the Bahamas in December 1962 Kennedy agreed that the British should be supplied with three Polaris submarines [13]. France received a similar offer which de Gaulle rejected. He also twice vetoed British membership of the EEC (in 1963 and 1968).

The United States sought to satisfy European aspirations for some say in nuclear weapons by setting up in March 1963 a multilateral fleet (MLF) of twenty-five surface ships carrying Polaris missiles, which would be manned by sailors from several NATO countries. This led to anxious enquiries by Moscow as to whether the MLF would give West Germany access to nuclear weapons. For its part France refused to participate, not only on the grounds that the whole scheme was operationally unsound, but also because Washington still insisted on the ultimate veto on the use of the nuclear weapon. The Johnson administration abandoned the scheme. France (and China) also refused to sign the Test Ban Treaty and attacked it as a blatant attempt by the Soviet Union and the United States to preserve their nuclear duopoly while denying other nations the opportunity to develop their own nuclear arsenals. Franco-American relations declined still further after 1962. During the Cuban missile crisis France supported the United States but de Gaulle resented the American failure to consult him prior to their quarantine decision.

During the late 1950s economic and military collaboration between France and West Germany marked a major turning point in the relations between those historic enemies. De Gaulle negotiated the Franco-German Treaty of Friendship of January 1963 – although the West German *Bundestag* was less ready to see a distancing from the US. By developing close ties with West Germany he hoped both to constrain West German power and enlist that power to strengthen France's independence from the United States. The French president bitterly attacked Johnson's handling of the Vietnam situation and in 1966 he withdrew France from military participation in NATO [13]. This forced the relocation of the NATO headquarters from Paris to Brussels. In that same year de Gaulle also raised the idea of détente. He visited Moscow in June 1966 and seemed to suggest the possibility of recognising the existence of two German states. His Foreign Minister, Couve de Murville, visited Warsaw, Bucharest, Budapest and Sofia in the spring and summer of 1966. 'De Gaulle was not only moving toward the East, he was also moving from the West, so to speak. Parallel with his movement towards détente with the East, in 1966 he loosened his ties with the Western alliance' [49: 124].

West Germany and European Détente

West Germany was also exploring new directions [57]. Konrad Adenauer was West Germany's Chancellor, 1949–1963. Under him the 'Hallstein Doctrine' applied: no recognition of East Germany and an ending of relations with any country, save the Soviet Union, which did recognise the East German regime. In October 1963 Adenauer resigned and was replaced by Ludwig Erhard. In March 1966 Erhard's Christian Democrat (CDU)-Free Democrat (FDP) coalition government made approaches to Eastern Europe. A 'Peace Note' proposing an exchange of declarations not to use force in settling international disputes was sent to all East European states, except East Germany. It was rejected. Erhard established German trade missions in Romania, Bulgaria, Poland and Hungary. The momentum increased in December 1966 when the Social Democrats (SPD), which had always been more favourable to exploring openings to the East replaced the FDP in the coalition with Kurt Kiesinger as Chancellor. As early as July 1963 Egon Bahr, the party's foreign policy specialist, committed the SPD to developing diplomatic and economic links with Eastern Europe. Kiesinger immediately spoke of better relations and even the possibility of diplomatic relations with East European states. The 'Hallstein Doctrine' was dead. 'Perhaps the chief consequence of the Gaullist opening towards Eastern Europe was the pressure it brought on West Germany to follow suit' [37 : 273]. Willy Brandt was the leading proponent of these West German attempts at an opening with the East, first as Foreign Minister under Kiesinger and then as Chancellor of the first SPD government after 1969. In his memoirs he observed, 'We could not become the last of the Cold

Warriors, the opponents of change and thus, perhaps, the world's leading troublemakers (and whipping boys)' [17: 167].

The East Europeans also played a role in these developments. Albania moved closer to China. Romania, where Nicolae Ceausescu came to power in 1965, also, if to a lesser degree, edged towards China. It developed trading ties with Western Europe. In addition, it failed to toe the Soviet line. Ceausescu refused to sever diplomatic relations with Israel in 1967 and declined to join the Warsaw Pact invasion of Czechoslovakia in 1968. In Czechoslovakia there was the Prague spring in 1968 under Alexander Dubcek's liberal communist leadership. Dubcek aimed to separate party and state and to make government accountable to parliament. He hoped to be the leader of a communist dominated coalition. However, he underestimated how this might encourage more wide ranging criticism and so provoke a strong reaction from communist hardliners in Czechoslovakia, the rest of the Warsaw Pact and in Moscow [114].

The Sino-Soviet Split

The most significant development in the communist world, however, was the Sino-Soviet split. In 1957 Khrushchev promised to help the Chinese in their development of an atomic device. In 1959, however, he reneged on his undertaking, saying that the current talks on a test ban precluded the Soviets from fulfilling their commitment. It is probable that the real reason lay in Khrushchev's pursuit of détente with the United States. While Khrushchev spoke of 'peaceful engagement', Mao endorsed 'armed struggle' with capitalism. Personal animosity between the two communist leaders also exacerbated relations. In July 1960 their rupture became more explicit when Khrushchev secured the backing of eighty-one communist parties against China's foreign policy. Only Albania opposed the Soviet initiative. The dispute became worse in 1967 and centred on their long border. When the Chinese launched a live warhead in October 1966 and tested an H-Bomb in June 1967, the Soviets responded by building up their troops on the frontier. There was a series of clashes on the border in the course of 1967–1968 [96: 254–255, 323–324].

The Sino-Soviet rupture seemed to offer the prospect of a more flexible USSR at a time when US-Soviet tensions were easing and when the Europeans were also seeking dialogue with the Warsaw Pact. But such hopes were dashed as the Johnson administration became dominated after 1965 by its deepening involvement in Vietnam.

Vietnam, 1965–1968

Johnson was a firm believer in the 'domino theory' whereby, if South Vietnam fell to communism, the resulting loss of faith in the United States' determination to combat communism would destroy morale in the other Asian non-communist countries. The new president was soon faced with a major crisis in the Republic of (South) Vietnam (RVN), when, in December 1963, the hardliners in the Communist Party Central Committee in Hanoi pushed through a major expansion of the insurgency in the south. In 1964, with the increasing disintegration of the Army of the Republic of Vietnam (AVRN) and political chaos in Saigon, the North despatched regular troops of the Peoples' Army of Vietnam (PAVN) – the North Vietnamese Army – to reinforce the Viet Cong (the Vietnamese Communist guerrillas) with the aim of defeating the demoralised AVRN and the failing Republic of Vietnam and reuniting the country under the Hanoi dominated National Liberation Front (NLF). Hanoi believed that, as a result, Johnson would be forced to withdraw American military forces from South Vietnam. In fact the opposite took place. In the face of increasing Viet Cong activity in South Vietnam, the United States Joint Chiefs of Staff urged Johnson to authorise the bombing of North Vietnam's fledgling industrial centres and of the Ho Chi Minh Trail (named after the famous leader of the Peoples' Republic of Vietnam) to interdict the passage of men and supplies from the North to the Viet Cong. The opportunity to act on this advice was provided in early August 1964 when North Vietnamese torpedo boats attacked a US destroyer in the Gulf of Tonkin, which had been engaged in supporting clandestine South Vietnamese operations in the south of the Democratic Republic of (North) Vietnam (DRV). As a result of this attack Johnson ordered a retaliatory air strike on North Vietnam and secured from Congress the so-called Gulf of Tonkin resolution which gave the president the authority to retaliate against North Vietnam 'to repel any armed attack against the forces of the United States and to prevent further aggression'. This resolution was to provide the administration with Congressional authorisation for the bombing campaign against the North and the subsequent introduction of United States ground forces into South Vietnam – although it is doubtful whether many of its Congressional backers anticipated the scale of the military operations which were to ensue.

After his victory in the November 1964 presidential election, Johnson became even more determined to deal with the Viet Cong, believing that United States' intervention would be of a limited nature and of short duration. His resolution was encouraged by his Secretary of Defense, Robert McNamara, and his other political and military advisers who pressed him to act before the Viet Cong destroyed the Saigon regime whose forces were suffering defeat after defeat at the hands of the Viet Cong and the PAVN. There is a debate about whether JFK would have made the same commitment of ground forces. The majority of historians think that he would have done the same as LBJ. DeGroot feels Kennedy would have faced the same circumstances as Johnson, would have used the same logic and so would have reacted in the same way [29: 80]. For Schulzinger 'it is hard to believe that the United States would not have participated the way it did in Vietnam, at least until 1968' [103: 334]. Freedman accepts that the circumstances were worse in 1963 than in 1961 but he is less sure that Kennedy would have done the same as LBJ. There were fewer sceptics and more who favoured US military intervention in Johnson's administration. Kennedy was ready to re-consider the US presence, while LBJ was not. Moreover, 'unlike Johnson, he would have looked hard at methods by which he might have escaped from the commitment including negotiations with the North' [43: 400, 403, 413].

Johnson's reluctance to act decisively at this point has been attributed to his commitment to social reform at home – the Great Society programme – which he feared would be derailed by stepped up United States intervention in Vietnam which would divert resources from the Great Society and provide Congressional conservatives with the opportunity to oppose his reform programme. However the reality of the impending disaster in South Vietnam forced his hand. He felt that he could not face the political fall-out from a communist victory in South Vietnam which had dogged Harry Truman when the republicans accused the latter of 'losing' China in the late 1940s [50; 98]. Moreover, he concluded, as he said to Congress in October 1966, 'We are a rich Nation, and we can afford to make progress at home while meeting obligations abroad' [110: 189].

On 7 February 1965 the United States air base at Pleiku was attacked by the Viet Cong, killing and wounding American troops and destroying American airplanes. In retaliation Johnson ordered the beginning of a major bombing campaign against the North – 'Rolling Thunder' – in an effort at least to stabilise the military and political situation in South Vietnam by demonstrating to both the North and South Vietnamese and the international community of America's commitment to the continued existence of an independent South Vietnam. Johnson's advisers believed that this evidence of American determination would force North Vietnam to negotiate an end to its intervention in the South. With a small and rather primitive industrial infrastructure, and with weapons and equipment pouring into the DRV from Communist China and the Soviet Union, the DRV remained impervious to the bombing campaign throughout the Johnson presidency – the DRV did falter occasionally but the bombing strengthened the steadfastness of North Vietnamese people in continuing with the war. Hanoi now stepped up its military campaign in the south, destroying ARVN forces with impunity. The American commander of the Military Assistance Command, Vietnam (MACV), General William Westmoreland, urged the despatch of United States ground forces to halt the Viet Cong and by May 75,000 American troops were sent to South Vietnam to bolster the flagging AVRN forces. This number soon proved to be insufficient and in July Johnson sent a further 50,000 troops and authorised the aerial bombardment of Viet Cong controlled areas in the south. Heavy American troop reinforcements were subsequently despatched every year until 1968, when the total number of troops had expanded to 540,000. The AVRN was effectively sidelined by the American military, rightly contemptuous of its military capabilities. Unlike the United States Air Force,

Westmoreland was not fettered by Washington in his operational decisions, although he was not allowed to plan for a ground invasion of the North since this might trigger Chinese intervention. USAF bombing campaign over North Vietnam was monitored by Johnson and his civilian advisers. Targets in the North were carefully selected, at first to avoid heavy population centres and Hanoi and Haiphong – which might spark angry protests from domestic and international opinion. Gradually bombing restrictions in the North were relaxed, and industrial, fuel and transport facilities were, by 1967, being regularly targeted.

Westmoreland's military strategy in the South had little discernable effect either on the Viet Cong's ability to continue fighting, although it did change its tactics. Westmoreland's 'search and destroy' strategy was designed to root out and kill the Viet Cong in the areas of South Vietnam they had occupied. It was hoped that the Viet Cong effort was already being seriously weakened by the bombardment of North Vietnam and the supply routes to the south, a campaign designed to stem the passage of North Vietnamese weapons, food and men to the south. This strategy failed. The bombing of North Vietnam and the supply routes certainly had some effect on North Vietnam's morale but China opposed a premature peace while the communists in the South were determined to fight on, despite increasing northern concern about their heavy troop losses. In the event the supply routes were repaired and used by the Viet Cong during the night – and in any case they were difficult to hit accurately given the forested nature of the terrain. The Viet Cong now avoided large unit confrontations with the Americans, who, with their superiority in weaponry, usually prevailed against the more lightly armed Viet Cong. The latter now resorted to guerrilla attacks consisting of hit and run ambushes of American formations after which they (the Viet Cong) would disappear into the jungle. Once American troops had 'liberated' a Viet Cong controlled base area, they would then move on to the next objective, enabling the Viet Cong to return to the previously 'liberated 'area. The Americans never had sufficient front line troops available to adopt a 'search and hold' strategy. An 'enclave strategy', defending and pacifying coastal and heavily populated areas, was proposed by the marines but was only partially deployed, presumably because it assumed slower results [120: 336]. The success of 'search and destroy' methods was measured by the 'body count' of Viet Cong dead, but this method was crude and unreliable, often failing to distinguish between Viet Cong and South Vietnamese civilians killed during the fighting. The figures were also often inflated by overzealous US and AVRN commanders anxious to show their mettle. Contrary to American expectations that the communists would soon exhaust their manpower resources, the communists, thanks to their high birth rate, found little difficulty in replacing killed and injured Viet Cong guerillas by fresh conscripts. Moreover Communist China, after unofficial American assurances in 1965 that the United States would not invade North Vietnam, increased its supplies of weapons and equipment into North Vietnam and sent technicians and engineers to repair essential facilities damaged by the bombing – thus freeing more North Vietnamese for other tasks. The Soviet Union, locked in bitter acrimony with China, sought to keep the DRV on its side by supplying it with sophisticated anti-aircraft facilities and fighter planes which took an increasing toll of American bombers [50; 98].

By the end of 1967 Westmoreland had become convinced that his strategy in the south was succeeding – certainly the Viet Cong had lost large numbers of men during the campaign – and he made public statements to the effect that the insurgency would soon be eliminated. This refrain was taken up by the Johnson administration at home, anxious to demonstrate to the American anti-war movement, who were becoming increasingly vocal and visible by 1967 (a demonstration at the Pentagon in October attracted 30,000 protesters), and to the majority of Americans who continued to support the war, that victory was at hand. It was thus a considerable shock to Americans when, on 31 January 1968, the lunar new year holiday of Tet, the PAVN and the Viet Cong launched a major offensive in the south, seizing provincial capitals and towns and even penetrating into the US Embassy compound in Saigon – images of these events being shown to a bewildered American public in television news bulletins and press photographs. Hitherto, there had been little footage of combat – less than a quarter of film coverage 1965–1967 featured actual fighting. The object of this offensive was to stem Viet Cong losses by overthrowing the Saigon regime, encouraging a popular uprising in the south, and replacing it by a NLF government which would end the United States presence in the south and reunify Vietnam. The offensive was a devastating failure for the communists. There was no popular uprising in the south and US and AVRN forces soon recovered the imitative, crushing the Viet Cong in the towns and later the villages, inflicting 30,000 casualties. But the fact that the Tet offensive had taken place at all in the face of the Johnson administration's public optimism about the progress of the war, was a major blow to Johnson's credibility. There followed a major upsurge in public and congressional protests against continuation of the war. Johnson's close advisers, ('the Wise Men') led by a new Secretary of Defense, Clark Clifford (a disillusioned McNamara, convinced that the war was unwinnable, had recently resigned) and the former Secretary of State, Dean Acheson, informed Johnson that a favourable outcome of the war was unlikely. The economy was being severely damaged by the immense cost of the conflict, inflation was mounting and there were burgeoning budget and balance of payments deficits [50; 98]. By 1968 the war's annual cost was $25.2 billion [96: 283] and there was a federal budget deficit of $24.2 billion [110: 210].

As a result, in a sensational about-turn, Johnson refused General Westmoreland's request for further troop reinforcements and on 31 March announced that there would be a partial ending of the bombing of Vietnam, and that he would seek peace negotiations with the North Vietnamese. He also stated that he would not stand for re-election in November 1968. Peace talks were held in Paris from the spring of 1968 but made no progress – convinced that the United States was on the run, the DRV and the Viet Cong refused to make any concessions to the Americans and demanded the complete withdrawal of American forces and a change of government leading to the reunification of the country.

Exploring Détente

Events in Vietnam in 1968 provided an impetus for both the superpowers and for the Europeans to explore détente. America was under military pressure in Vietnam and in economic difficulties and was looking for relief. The Soviets saw this as their opportunity to benefit. They were further emboldened in pursuing this policy by having achieved approximate nuclear parity. By November 1969 the Soviet Union had more

ICBMs – 1140 to the US total of 1054 – but the Americans could add their nuclear bombers and submarine-launched missiles. [81: 123; 110: 213–216]. The Europeans were critical of American policy in Vietnam. Many Europeans wondered whether the preoccupation with Vietnam would undermine the American commitment to station ground troops in Western Europe and thus weaken NATO. From 1966 onwards Senator Mike Mansfield of Montana sponsored Senate resolutions favouring substantial cuts in US forces in Europe.

If Vietnam provided an opportunity, it was, for Garthoff, de Gaulle's moves that 'broke the ice and facilitated moves by others to thaw the frozen state of confrontation between East and West in Europe' [49: *124*]. His initiatives provoked a reassessment of the West's Cold War policies. In December 1966 the Belgian Prime Minister, Pierre Harmel, persuaded NATO to commission a study group to prepare a report, 'The Future Tasks of the Alliance'. In what came to be known as the Harmel Report he argued for the pursuit of a relaxation of tensions, détente, and for an alliance that remained strong. On 14 December 1967 NATO endorsed the Report. Its adoption led to the first studies by NATO of force reductions in Europe in 1968–1970 [49: 127–128]. At a ministerial meeting in Reykjavik, Iceland, in June 1968, NATO declared its readiness to 'explore with other interested states specific and practical steps in the arms control field', and proposed talks on mutual force reductions. This was the first move towards the negotiations on mutual and balanced force reductions (MBFR), which eventually began in 1973.

Europe's moves helped edge the US towards détente. President Johnson considered ways of easing East–West tensions. On 7 October 1966 he gave a speech, drafted by Zbigniew Brzezinski (later to be President Carter's National Security Adviser, 1977–1981) suggesting that the two superpowers seek a 'peaceful engagement' with Eastern Europe. In June 1967 LBJ and the Soviet Premier, Alexei Kosygin, met in Glassboro, New Jersey. In the course of their meeting they made the tentative first steps towards a possible treaty limiting their strategic nuclear weapons. The Johnson administration also began to explore non-proliferation. In July 1968 the United States and the Soviet Union signed the Non-Proliferation Treaty. By 1985 some 131 countries had ratified it. In addition, they agreed to talks on a Strategic Arms

Limitation Treaty (SALT). Efforts were also made to seek an Anti-ABM (Anti-Ballistic Missile) agreement.

Conclusion

East–West relations had witnessed a pitch of intensity in 1961–1962 with the abortive invasion of Cuba, a crisis over Berlin and fear of nuclear war over Soviet missiles in Cuba. But the aftermath offered the promise of a better atmosphere, bringing as it did the Test Ban Treaty, the Non-Proliferation Treaty and the discussions on SALT and ABM systems. Meanwhile in Europe first France, then West Germany sought détente with Eastern Europe. Vietnam, however, cast a growing shadow and distraction for the Americans. Then there came the Soviet invasion of Czechoslovakia in August 1968, which crushed Dubcek's liberal communism. It halted negotiations on SALT and moves towards an Anti-ABM Treaty, as well as delaying the beginning of MBFR talks. The LBJ–Kosygin summit, planned for November, was cancelled. Although Brezhnev's speech in November to the Polish Communist Party articulated the principle of justified intervention to restore socialism, what became known as the Brezhnev Doctrine, Soviet action against the Czechs did not prove an insuperable obstacle. Further progress, however, would have to await the outcome of the US presidential election in November 1968.

5 The Cold War Declines, 1969–1976

Nixon and Kissinger

When Richard M. Nixon won the November 1968 presidential election, he appointed Henry Kissinger as his National Security Adviser. This unlikely partnership was to dominate US foreign policy between 1969 and 1974. Yet they came from such different backgrounds. Nixon was a poor Quaker from California who paid his way through college. After qualifying as a lawyer and service in the navy during the war, he was elected to Congress in 1946 and then to the Senate in 1950 where he made a name for himself as an ardent anti-communist. He served as Eisenhower's Vice-President from 1953 to 1961 but lost the 1961 election to John Kennedy. Kissinger was a Jewish refugee from Germany. After wartime service in the US army, he enjoyed a brilliant academic career at Harvard: a summa cum laude degree was followed by a PhD on the 'congress system' after the Napoleonic wars and rapid promotion to full professor by 1960. He gained international recognition with his book, *Nuclear Weapons and Foreign Policy* (1957), and established a network of political connexions while serving as director of the Harvard international seminar. Nixon liked the idea of having a well-regarded intellectual in the White House, while Kissinger was attracted to power, to shaping policy and not just analysing it. Although they never saw themselves as friends, they did have certain things in common. They shared difficult backgrounds and a sense that they were outside the establishment; they were loners and were fascinated by history; they were firmly anti-communist and favoured tough realpolitik; and they were comfortable with secret diplomacy concentrated in the White House.

Another thing they had in common was their concern about how bureaucratic rivalry had hindered US foreign policy since the war. The National Security Act (1947) had, in theory, given the president control of foreign policy but had not removed rivalry between agencies. Kissinger proposed to Nixon that the National Security Adviser should become 'the principal forum for issues requiring inter-agency co-ordination'. From the first day Kissinger assumed control of the planning function of NSC by requiring in the president's name that policy papers be cleared by him and his staff. He inundated the State Department and the Departments of Defense and the Treasury with demands for information. He created special working groups to co-ordinate policies on Vietnam, South Africa and the Middle East [102: 291–292]. William P. Rogers was appointed Secretary of State and provided the administration with a public image of integrity but he was effectively sidelined. Eventually, in September 1973, Kissinger replaced Rogers as Secretary of State while retaining the post of National Security Adviser. Although Kissinger thus accumulated a great deal of power in the administration, there was never any doubt that Nixon was in charge. Moreover, the President was often the instigator of the more innovative initiatives like the opening of relations with communist China.

In their geopolitical vision Nixon and Kissinger placed less emphasis on ideology. They no longer regarded communism's ideological appeal as a danger. It was Soviet power that concerned them. Kissinger's PhD had focused on the balance of power after 1815. Seeing himself as a latter-day Metternich, he thought he could achieve a similar balance of power between the two superpowers now that the Soviet Union had acquired nuclear parity. Their first priority was Vietnam. In particular they wanted to silence the domestic criticism. They aimed to achieve this by reducing the number of US troops in Vietnam and by exploiting Sino-Soviet tensions. Nixon hoped to remove Chinese and Soviet support for North Vietnam, a price they might be willing to pay for better relations with the United States, thereby making Hanoi more amenable to a peace settlement [7; 101].

Ostpolitik

West Germany was also seeking a new basis for its relations with the East, what became known as *Ostpolitik* (Eastern policy). In October 1969 Willy Brandt was elected as its first Socialist (SPD) Chancellor in a coalition with the FDP. He immediately revived and intensified his efforts towards détente during his time as Foreign Minister in the preceding Kiesinger government. According to Martin Walker, Europe had a particular agenda for détente which 'involved a degree of self-liberation from the tutelage of the dominant super-powers' [110: 219]. European détente focused on issues that were different from those between the US and the USSR; it was concerned not with nuclear weapons but with cultivating various economic and cultural inter-changes between East and West and formalising borders. Moreover, European détente was more enduring, beginning in the 1960s and continuing until the 1980s. It seems clear that the Soviet Union wished to encourage détente in Western Europe. In March 1969 the Warsaw Pact again suggested a conference on European security and co-operation.

In November 1969 Brandt signed the Nuclear Non-Proliferation Treaty, thereby allaying Warsaw Pact fears of a nuclear West Germany. He made clear his desire to open diplomatic relations with Poland and to reach an understanding with East Germany. But first he pursued an agreement with the Soviet Union. Talks began in December 1969 and resulted in the West Germany–USSR Non-Aggression Pact, which he signed in Moscow in August 1970. Brandt next turned to Poland, signing a treaty in December 1970 that recognised the Oder–Neisse frontier between the two countries and renounced any future territorial claims. Poland also agreed to improve its treatment of the German minority within its borders. But what made the agreement memorable was Brandt's request for pardon as he knelt at the memorial to the Warsaw Ghetto. Finally, Brandt sought to negotiate with East Germany. In January 1970 he proposed a non-aggression pact between the two German states but the offer did not involve full diplomatic recognition and so was rejected by East Germany. Talks between Brandt and the East German prime minister, Willi Stolph, were cordial but unproductive. It was only when Walter Ulbricht, Communist Party leader in East Germany, resigned in May 1971 that there was real progress. He was replaced by the more flexible Erich Honecker. It seems likely that the change in leadership came as a result of Soviet pressure.

These negotiations were running in parallel with talks, which began in March 1970, between the four occupying powers (Britain, France, the Soviet Union and the United States) on Berlin. The central issue was the continued Western presence there. The Soviet Union sought to remove or, at least, greatly reduce the links between West Berlin and West Germany, while the Western powers were determined to retain their presence and access to Berlin. There was one difficulty in the West's position: the four occupying powers could not recognise West German authority in West Berlin, because to do so would undermine their own.

Brandt was determined to get an agreement on Berlin before ratifying the Moscow and Warsaw Treaties. His aim was to win concessions from the USSR on Berlin in return for his acceptance of Germany's post-1945 borders. The Berlin Agreement of 3 September 1971 was finally achieved through confidential American (White House)–Soviet conversations which were then agreed by the four powers' ambassadors. Although it only recognised the status quo, the agreement was still significant. It guaranteed Western access to the city, thereby lessening the likelihood of another blockade like that in 1948–1949. The Soviets recognised the legitimacy of political ties between Berlin and Bonn while Brandt agreed to reduce West Germany's political role in Berlin and abandoned his hopes of integrating the city into West Germany. The West recognised East Germany (GDR) and the Soviets accepted the continuation of the four powers' responsibilities for Berlin. In December 1971 a GDR-West German transit agreement on access to West Berlin was reached. In May 1972 there was a broader Traffic Treaty. Finally, in December 1972 a 'Treaty on the Bases of Relations' was concluded. The December treaty extended recognition by each German state to the other, renounced the use of force and committed them to increased trade and travel between the two countries [17; 57; 49: 125–126, 135–139; 68].

The Americans were rather wary of Brandt's *Ostpolitik*, fearing it would give the Soviet Union leverage over West Germany and so the other European allies. In his memoirs Kissinger noted that Nixon and he were moved to develop an American détente with the Soviet Union in part to preclude a West German-led

European détente with the Soviet Union which excluded the United States, thus splitting the Western alliance [68: 410–411, 529–531; 69: 145–146]. But they came to see the value of the policy and, in any case, could have done little to prevent it without causing a diplomatic crisis. Moreover, Brandt's policies had benefits for connected issues. West Germany wanted an agreement on Berlin and used ratification of the Warsaw and Moscow treaties and the prospect of recognising the GDR as bargaining counters. The Soviet Union was pliable on Berlin because it wanted agreement on the Oder–Neisse frontier and recognition of East Germany and NATO's agreement to a European security conference. The United States had long wanted a Berlin settlement. Each country achieved its desiderata: Berlin was settled, the treaties were ratified and NATO was willing to attend a European security conference.

Ending the Vietnam War, 1969–1973

For all their initial caution about *Ostpolitik*, Nixon and Kissinger were pleased with its results, especially on Berlin. But their priority remained Vietnam. Indeed, Nixon came to office with a commitment to end America's involvement in the war. This did not mean, however, that the new president would accept defeat in Vietnam – an outcome which would prejudice America's global prestige which Nixon was as determined to uphold as Johnson had been. But he accepted that America's role as the 'world policeman' would have to be reduced. The new approach was articulated in July 1969 and became known as the 'Nixon Doctrine'. Although America would deploy air and naval power to uphold its treaty responsibilities in the Western Pacific, Asian troops would now have to shoulder the main burden on the ground as American troops were withdrawn.

Nixon and Kissinger pursued a threefold strategy. First, there would be successive withdrawals of US troops from Vietnam – numbers fell from approximately 540,000 in 1969 to roughly 160,000 in December 1971 [120: 343; 37: 259]. Secondly, the administration increased military aid to South Vietnam to reinforce this Vietnamisation policy. In 1969 the Americans sent $1 billion of weapons and matériel to South Vietnam [101: 34]. Thirdly, and most ambitiously, they pursued what has become known as 'triangular diplomacy', playing off the Soviet Union and China against one another to strengthen the American negotiating position with North Vietnam.

Vietnamisation involved the gradual withdrawal of all American ground troops and the South Vietnamese forces (AVRN) assuming their role on the ground. To enable the AVRN to be expanded, trained and equipped – a process which would take time – the Americans planned to undertake a number of initiatives which would keep the North Vietnamese and Viet Cong on the defensive. In March 1969 a heavy bombing campaign by the USAF against neutral Cambodia was inaugurated in order to destroy Viet Cong–North Vietnamese (PAVN) bases there. It lasted for fourteen months and was somehow kept secret from the American news media. This was followed in April 1970 by a joint AVRN-US military expedition into Cambodia to destroy communist sanctuaries and to impede alleged communist preparations for an offensive into South Vietnam. There was an immediate outcry in the United States when the president announced the invasion, and Congress was given the opportunity to recover the power it had ceded to Johnson in 1964. Nixon was forced by legislation to withdraw the invasion force from Cambodia by 1 July 1970, and the Gulf of Tonkin resolution was revoked.

During the latter stages of Johnson's presidency the previously volatile political situation in Saigon had stabilised under the dictatorship of General Nguyen Van Thieu. The Americans now encouraged Thieu to embark on a rural pacification programme, designed to provide the population with medical and educational facilities – previous half-hearted efforts in this direction had become mired in corruption and administrative incompetence. Thieu's army numbered about a million men but militarily its quality was highly suspect, as was demonstrated when an AVRN invasion of Laos between January and March 1971, approved by the American Military Command and supported by American artillery and airpower (but not ground troops), turned into a major disaster, with the AVRN forced into headlong retreat by the North Vietnamese army. Nixon and Kissinger concluded that Vietnamisation was not working and turned to the peace talks in Paris between the US, North Vietnam, the Provisional Revolutionary Government of South Vietnam and the Republic of Vietnam as a way out of the morass.

Formal peace negotiations began in Paris in January 1969 and continued in weekly meetings over the next four years. These were no more than exchanges of propaganda, the real talks being held in secret. In August 1969 Kissinger had begun to engage in a series of meetings with senior North Vietnamese leaders. Although Nixon and Kissinger sought a total US withdrawal eventually, they were not ready to accept defeat in Vietnam. Frank Snepp has suggested that they favoured a settlement that would provide a respectable fig leaf for US withdrawal, allowing a 'decent interval' between American withdrawal and South Vietnam's collapse. But most historians believe that Nixon wanted a non-communist South Vietnam. Nixon aimed to keep the North Vietnamese guessing. He deliberately cultivated an air of unpredictability and a readiness to use force, as witnessed in the invasions of Cambodia in June 1970 and of Laos in July 1971, the mining of Haiphong in May 1972 and the large-scale bombing of North Vietnam in December 1972. In this way he hoped to strengthen Kissinger's hand in the secret negotiations with North Vietnam. In 1969–1970 Kissinger held twelve secret meetings with Le Duc Tho, the chief North Vietnamese negotiator. These meetings were made public in late 1970. Further negotiations in 1971–1972 were reported but the details were not revealed. There was hardly any meeting of minds, until, in May 1971, Kissinger told, Le Duc Tho, that the United States was now willing to accept a cease fire whereby South and North Vietnamese forces would remain in their existing positions in South Vietnam while the United States would withdraw its forces from the country in return for Hanoi's repatriation of American prisoners-of-war. This was a considerable advance on previous American offers since hitherto Kissinger had insisted that United States and North Vietnamese forces should both withdraw from the south at the same time. The North Vietnamese countered that Thieu must leave office – a step too far for the Americans.

With the failure of the South Vietnamese military to defeat the North Vietnamese in Laos and the stalemated Paris talks Nixon and Kissinger hoped that the opening to China and détente with the Soviet Union [see pp. 110–111] would encourage both powers to put pressure on the North Vietnamese to reach a compromise with the United States in South Vietnam. But despite expressions of good will by both the Soviet and Chinese leaders, little was achieved since neither China nor the Soviet Union, locked in a 'cold war' of their own, wanted to alienate a likely ally. Indeed Soviet supplies to North Vietnam increased during the early 1970s. By 1972 the North Vietnamese believed that their re-equipped and re-trained army would make short work of the AVRN, now bereft of United States ground support. In March 1972 120,000 North Vietnamese forces, supported by the Viet Cong, launched a major offensive into South Vietnam. At first it enjoyed considerable success but in April Nixon ordered massive aerial attacks on North Vietnam, particularly on targets like Haiphong, which Johnson had exempted from attack. Together with air attacks against the PAVN and its supply routes in the south and in Laos, the North was forced to call off its assault, having sustained heavy losses. Now Hanoi returned to the negotiating table at Paris, offering concessions to the Americans which included the retention of Thieu as president. A draft agreement in October 1972 between Kissinger and Le Duc Tho provided for a complete American pullout of their remaining air, land and naval forces from Vietnam, a ceasefire in the South which would leave North and South Vietnamese forces in their existing positions in the south and the holding later of democratic elections which would determine whether South Vietnam remained independent or would reunite with the North. However Thieu denounced the draft treaty and, despite American promises of increased military and post-war aid, refused to change his mind. Increasingly frustrated, Nixon ordered the resumption of the bombing of North Vietnam – it had been suspended during the peace talks – which began in December and was only brought to a halt at the end of the month when the North Vietnamese agreed to return to Paris. The bombing campaign was intended to demonstrate both to Thieu and to the North Vietnamese what the United States could do if the terms of a peace treaty were broken by the North. It certainly convinced Thieu of the likely massive retaliation by the United States if the North violated the settlement and he finally agreed to sign the final peace treaty in Paris on 23 January 1973, which was unchanged from the provisional agreement reached by Kissinger and Le Duc Tho in October. So ended a war that had cost American 58,000 lives and maybe two million Vietnamese deaths [50; 98; 103; 29].

China

Nixon and Kissinger realised that the Sino-Soviet split – there was serious fighting on the Usurri River between March and September 1969 – offered a major diplomatic opportunity for the United States. Nixon concluded that better US-Chinese relations might allow him to use China as a lever against the Soviet Union. As Kissinger said, 'The hostility between China and the Soviet Union served our purposes best if we maintained closer relations with each side than they did with each other. The rest could be left to the dynamics of events' [68: 712]. Nixon correctly surmised that Chinese worries about Soviet intentions made them responsive to US approaches. In July 1969 the State Department removed the requirement for US students and scholars travelling to China to obtain special permission for their trips. In October the US Ambassador to Poland was instructed to contact a senior Chinese official and suggest conversations between Chinese and American diplomats in Warsaw. Then in January 1970 the US Ambassador agreed to meet Chinese diplomats at their mission, referring to it for the first time as the 'Embassy of the People's Republic of China'. China responded in kind. On 1 October 1970 an American journalist, Edgar Snow, was invited to join the National Day celebrations in Peking. Mao spoke to him pessimistically of the Sino-Soviet conflict and more optimistically of America. In April 1971, in a very public signal, the Chinese invited the American table tennis team to play in China. Meanwhile, there were secret exchanges through Pakistan which resulted in an invitation by the Chinese in April 1971 for the United States to send an envoy to Beijing. Kissinger travelled to Pakistan in July 1971 and, feigning illness, spent two days as the US envoy in Beijing where the Chinese invited Nixon to visit China. On Kissinger's return Nixon made a television announcement of his acceptance of the invitation to an astonished US public. In October 1971 communist China was admitted to the UN and, although the US had wanted to retain a General Assembly seat for Taiwan, the replacement of the Nationalist delegation to the UN by the communist delegation removed a long-standing obstacle in the path of better US-Chinese relations.

Nixon's February 1972 visit to China was an outstanding success, though this was largely symbolic. It removed the bitter character to Sino-American relations which had prevailed since Mao's communists came to power in China in October 1949. There was also the difficult matter of what to do about Taiwan. This was resolved by devising a diplomatic formula acknowledging the Chinese claim to Taiwan and declaring the wish to seek a peaceful settlement of the question. Kissinger visited Beijing again in 1973 and set up an American liaison office which, in effect, was a US embassy. On this foundation US-Chinese relations saw nearly two decades of improving relations.

Nixon undoubtedly deserves the major credit for this achieve-ment. He conceived the idea and played an important part in its implementation. But he had an advantage in pursuing this policy. His fierce anti-communism undercut accusations by the political right in America that he was being soft on communism, a charge that would almost certainly have defeated such a policy by a liberal Democratic president. Yet, for all its benefits for Sino-American relations, Nixon's main objective was not to support China against the Soviet Union but to encourage a more accommodating attitude by the Soviet Union towards the United States [23; 84; 68].

The new relationship with China led Nixon and Kissinger to alter their outlook on Indo-Pakistan tensions. In 1971 the Bengalis of East Pakistan revolted against their military oppression by West Pakistan. The US government ignored the violent response of the Pakistani government. Indeed, when India intervened on behalf of the Bengalis, the White House, despite strong opposition from the State Department, sided with Pakistan. The Americans halted aid to India, sent weapons to Pakistan and dispatched a naval task force to the Bay of Bengal. This was done because Pakistan was valuable to Washington for the bases it permitted for U2 flights over the Soviet Union, for the facilities it allowed for the monitoring of Soviet nuclear tests, and because it had been a staging post for Kissinger's trip to China. Kissinger declared, 'we can't allow a friend of ours [Pakistan] and China's to get screwed in a conflict with a friend of Russia's [India]'. He regarded India, who had signed a treaty of friendship with Moscow in August 1971, as acting under Soviet advice. There was scant evidence for this. In addition, both he and the president wanted to demonstrate to China that America could be trusted in a crisis. Despite heated exchanges on the US-Soviet hot line, détente was not derailed [120: 371; 92: 436–437].

Soviet Union and Strategic Arms Limitation Talks

While there were startling developments in US-Chinese relations, there had been little progress in the US-Soviet relationship. SALT talks had first been raised by Johnson. Nixon at first reviewed the situation. Then, in June 1969, he instructed Rogers to tell the Soviet Ambassador to Washington, Dobrynin, that America was ready to open SALT talks in July. But the Soviets prevaricated. In November–December 1969 there was a preliminary meeting in Helsinki. The opening of diplomatic relations between the United States and China, however, made the Soviet Union readier to negotiate seriously. In four summit meetings between 1972 and 1974 – Moscow, May 1972, Washington DC, June 1973, Moscow, June–July 1974, Vladivostock, November 1974 – Nixon (then Gerald Ford in November 1974) and Brezhnev discussed a range of important issues from arms control to trade, from cultural, scientific and educational ties to a Basic Principles Agreement. The most important were two arms agreements – SALT I and the Anti-ABM Treaty.

At the May 1972 summit in Moscow Nixon and Brezhnev signed the SALT I agreement on strategic nuclear weapons. There would be a five-year freeze on US and Soviet missile launchers: 1054 American ICBMs to 1618 Soviet ones; 656 American Submarine-launched Ballistic Missiles (SLBMs) to 740 Soviet ones; and 455 American long-range bombers to 140 Soviet ones. Nixon accepted a deal that seemingly gave the Soviet Union superiority because the Americans, though having fewer ICBMs and SLBMs, had developed Multiple Independently Targetable Re-entry Vehicles (MIRVs) and so possessed an estimated three to one superiority in warheads. Unfortunately for arms control, since MIRVs were not included in SALT I, the Soviets began developing their own. There was an arms race in this area. So SALT I did not produce any significant reduction in armaments. Rather, it offered the prospect of being able to pursue this in the future.

The second agreement was the Anti-ABM Treaty. In the late 1960s the Soviet Union had established an ABM system around Moscow and at one of its main ICBM sites. At the same time the Americans had debated the possibility of developing their own defensive screen but doubts about its viability persisted. When the US Senate approved an ABM system by one vote it appeared to be doing so as a negotiating ploy in order to secure a treaty with the USSR. The agreement signed at the Moscow summit allowed two ABM systems for each country – around Moscow and Washington and a selected missile site. There would be a screen of 100 anti-ballistic missiles [10; 49].

The Moscow summit also saw the signature of a Joint Declaration on Basic Principles, by which the two countries undertook to consult one another so as to prevent an escalation of tensions leading to a military confrontation and possible war. A number of economic agreements were also reached in principle. The Wheat Sales Agreement of July 1972 allowed the Soviet Union to buy US grain worth $750 million over three years. In October 1972 the Soviet–American Trade Agreement was signed which included the extension of Most Favoured Nation status to the Soviet Union. In addition, a lend-lease settlement was achieved at the Moscow summit: the Soviet Union would pay $740 million over thirty years for the civilian goods sent to them during the Second World War. The main value of these agreements was not economic, but political. SALT I was to run for five years. The aim was to seek an improved agreement in SALT II talks. As Nixon put it in his memoirs, 'This was the first stage of détente: to involve Soviet interests in ways that would increase their stake in international stability and the status quo' [84: 618].

Chile, 1973

Progress in détente did not preclude difficulties in other parts of the world. American involvement in Latin America had long centred on military intervention. But the Kennedy administration realised something more was needed in the long term. So in March 1961 JFK announced the *Alliance for Progress*, a kind of Latin American Marshall Plan. It was launched in August 1961 with the commitment of $20 billion of US money. Participating countries had to match US aid with equal sums of their own. For all the fanfare it failed to produce any significant shift in relations between the United States and Latin America. A major problem centred on vested interests in these countries with little incentive to encourage reforms that were likely to reduce their hold on power and hinder their businesses. As a result, the US had to stop tying aid to political reform and make arrangements with the local elites. So corruption became even more of a problem. The high expectations and slender results of the *Alliance* did little to lessen the burgeoning revolutionary forces in a decade of rapid population increase. Both the local regimes and the US responded with force to the revolutionary movements. In 1965 LBJ sent marines into the Dominican Republic to prevent a civil war and put a junta temporarily in power, to be followed by elections.

So Nixon inherited a return to 'gunboat diplomacy' but at a time when there was reluctance to get bogged down in another foreign territory. He soon faced a problem in another South American state – Chile. But there was clear reticence about sending troops when Salvador Allende, leader of the Unidad Popular movement that was supported by both communists and socialists, was elected president in 1970. Allende gained 36.6 per cent of the votes to the right wing Nationalist Party's Jorge Allesandro's 43.9 per cent and the centrist Christian Democrats' Randomiro Tomic's 27.8 per cent. He therefore lacked a majority but the Chilean National Congress, following established tradition, confirmed him as president in October 1970.

The Nixon administration was outraged. It halted economic aid and gave generous funding to Allende's opponents. Then, on 11 September 1973, the military seized power. There is still a debate about what happened. But it is clear that Allende erred in failing to reach an understanding with the Christian Democrats and in imposing nationalisation and redistribution of wealth so abruptly. This antagonised the middle class and damaged the economy which experienced rising inflation and frequent strikes. So the military claimed to have intervened to save the country. There was clearly substantial American clandestine action against Allende. In 1970 Nixon and Kissinger had sought to prevent Allende's election, wanting to avoid 'another Cuba'. Nixon faced lobbying from US businesses who feared their assets would be nationalised. Yet a Senate committee in 1975 'found no evidence' that the United States 'was *directly* involved, covertly, in the 1973 coup in Chile', though it hinted at sympathy with the military coup. Headed by August Pinochet, the junta launched a brutal crackdown to rid Chile of Marxism. At least 3000 Chileans and some foreigners were killed or disappeared, scores of others were detained and tortured. What worried Kissinger and Nixon was that a successful socialist government in Chile might encourage others in Latin America to follow the same course. It seems they wanted to prevent the spread of socialist governments in the region [102; 14; 96].

Yom Kippur

The creation of the state of Israel in 1948 had produced a bitter and continuing regional dispute between it and its Arab neighbours, Egypt, Syria and Jordan. Wars in 1948–1949, in 1956 and in 1967 had seen Israeli victories. The June 1967 victory was especially painful for Arabs, as it saw Israel gain the Golan Heights from Syria and Sinai from Egypt. It was likely that at some stage there would be an attempt to regain these territories. In September 1970 Anwar Sadat became Egyptian leader after the death of Nasser. In July 1972 he dismissed Soviet military advisers. He probably did so to satisfy domestic critics and to win support from conservative Arab states, in particular oil-rich Saudi Arabia. He also hoped to gain a more sympathetic attitude from Washington. The Nixon administration, however, was preoccupied with a domestic crisis, the Watergate affair. Disappointed by this rebuff, Sadat now planned a war with Syria against Israel. By October 1972 Soviet military advisers were back in Cairo offering better military equipment, in particular surface to air missiles (SAMs) to deal with the Israeli air force. The Soviets, however, counselled against war. Despite the clear preparations for war by both the Syrians and Egyptians, the Americans failed to recognise the imminence of conflict partly because of the distractions of Watergate and partly because of their low opinion of these two countries' military forces.

The attack on 6 October 1973 fell on Yom Kippur, the Jewish Day of Atonement, and came as a great shock. Initially, it produced defeats for Israel. In the North the Syrians regained the Golan Heights, while in the Sinai the Egyptians smashed the Israeli defensive line and advanced into Israeli territory. But the Israelis led by General Elazar counter-attacked against Syria on 8–10 October, recapturing the Golan Heights after fierce fighting, and against Egypt on 14 October in the biggest tank battle since Kursk in 1943. Again the Israelis were victorious. Washington and Moscow tried to broker a ceasefire, sponsoring, on 22 October,

UN Security Council Resolution 338 that urged talks to achieve a peace settlement. Brezhnev suggested to Nixon that they should send military forces to ensure the UN resolution was implemented. He added that, if the US would not act jointly then the Soviet Union would consider acting unilaterally. It is likely that this was only a device to press the Americans to act, that Brezhnev had no intention of committing Soviet forces. However, this was not how Nixon and Kissinger interpreted the message. On 24 October the United States' forces around the world were placed on Defence Condition III, the highest state of preparedness short of war. This did not develop into a more serious crisis partly because the fighting ended and partly because of Brezhnev's restraint – he felt Nixon was 'too nervous – let's cool him down' [96: 375]. Yet for a while it was the most serious episode of US-Soviet tension since the Cuban missile crisis. The Middle East had become a vital region for the United States. Its growing need of oil from the area was emphasised when the Organisation of Petroleum Exporting Countries (OPEC) supported the Egyptians and Syrians by raising the price of oil by 70 per cent and imposing a boycott on the United States. Kissinger, meanwhile, used 'shuttle diplomacy', flying between Cairo and Tel Aviv and Damascus, and secured disengagement agreements for the Sinai and Golan by May 1974. As a result, OPEC removed its oil embargo [102; 69].

Watergate

American policy on the Yom Kippur War was undoubtedly hampered by a major crisis assailing the administration. On 17 June 1972 burglars entered the Democratic Party's national headquarters in the Watergate building in Washington DC and placed bugging devices. Nixon almost certainly did not order or even know about the burglary. But the break in was a consequence of earlier actions. In June 1971 Daniel Ellsberg had given the *New York Times* a copy of the secret Pentagon history of the Vietnam War. John Erhlichman, special assistant to the president, set up a team known as the 'plumbers' to plug further leaks. It was soon organising a variety of operations, including the Watergate burglary. The issue was kept out of the news until after the November 1972 presidential election. But, by early 1973, the burglars decided to talk in the hope of reduced sentences. In February a Senate Committee, chaired by Sam Ervin, was established. Its hearings began in May and soon it received evidence harmful to Nixon. At the same time, a Special Prosecutor, Archibald Cox, began collecting information. In July a White House aide revealed that Nixon taped his conversations. What followed was a dogged pursuit of these recordings by Congress and a rearguard action by Nixon. He sacked Cox in October. The progressive release of the tapes undermined the administration. In July 1974 the Supreme Court compelled Nixon to hand over tapes incriminating him in a cover up. One transcript contained Nixon's order to his Chief of Staff, H.R. Haldeman, to arrange for the CIA to halt the FBI inquiry into the Watergate burglary. Facing the likelihood of impeachment by Congress, he chose, instead, to resign on 9 August [38]. Kissinger has argued, 'His [Nixon's] administrative approach was weird and its human cost unattractive, yet history must also record the fundamental fact that major successes were achieved that had proved unattainable by conventional procedures' [68: 841]. It is certainly right to say that such methods secured some impressive achievements. Yet, as Garthoff says, 'The decline of détente and the subsequent problems and failures in sustaining a number of these major successes suggest that had they been attained through more conventional procedures and less by sleight of hand, they might have had greater staying power' [49: 349].

President Ford

Gerald R. Ford succeeded Richard Nixon as president. After twenty-five years in Congress, he became Vice-President in October 1973 when Spiro T. Agnew had resigned to avoid being prosecuted for taking bribes. He was a decent man who was far from the stumbling figure of popular opinion. But the full pardon he gave to Nixon hurt his popularity, encouraging the suspicion of a prior deal. He was a transitional figure. Although a conservative Republican, he believed in government power, in raising taxes on the wealthiest in the nation, in funding investment in highways, bridges, and schools. Such a programme was to be abandoned by the Republicans of Ronald Reagan in the 1980s. Ford did not challenge Kissinger's dominance of foreign policy. But it was his misfortune that his presidency witnessed the breakdown of the Vietnam peace settlement, as the communists conquered South Vietnam, and the decline of détente in the face of problems in Africa, an impasse over SALT II and domestic criticism. Even the Helsinki Accords brought accusations of appeasing the Soviet Union.

The Defeat of South Vietnam

No sooner had the January 1973 treaty been signed than both sides were violating the agreement. Thieu's South Vietnamese forces seized communist held areas of the country and the North sent troops and supplies to the south, despite its pledges in the treaty not to do so, to prepare for a renewed offensive. Events in the United States resulting from the fallout from Watergate played into North Vietnam's hands. Congress now blocked funding for any American military action in Indochina, made deep cuts in military aid to South Vietnam and insisted that the president consult Congress before authorising the despatch of American troops into battle. With effect from August 1973 Congress banned any military operations over Indochina. In November 1973 the War Powers Act put a sixty-day limit on troop deployments overseas without Congressional consent. Military aid to South Vietnam was cut by Congress from $2.3 billion in 1973 to $700 million by November 1974. Now the Democratic Republic of Vietnam could invade the south with impunity, which it did in January 1974 forcing the AVRN into headlong retreat. Thieu appealed to President Ford for American aid, but Ford was reluctant to become involved in renewed intervention in Vietnam and Congress refused the funding. On 30 April 1975 Saigon was occupied by the North Vietnam army, Thieu having fled the country ten days earlier. A year later the country was reunified under a communist government. It was a severe defeat for the United States which had, throughout the conflict, severely underestimated the determination and willpower of its communist adversary in Vietnam. What to the United States had been 'a limited war' had been a 'total war' for the North Vietnamese who were prepared to go to the limits of endurance to win [50; 98]. Cambodia had come under communist control in January 1975. When the communists took power in Laos in August the whole of Indochina was in communist hands.

Angola, 1974–1976

If the Americans could pursue their interests in Chile – the Soviets assumed American involvement in the coup against Allende – and take a prominent role in the Middle East, then, the Soviets concluded, détente need not apply outside Europe. In 1974 they decided to pursue their interests in Africa. In April 1974 a military coup in Lisbon overthrew Caetano, the successor of Salazar. It marked the end of the Portuguese empire. Mozambique moved to independence relatively smoothly because those who had been fighting for independence were largely united. Angola proved altogether more troublesome. Granted independence in November 1975, there followed a civil war involving the National Front for the Liberation of Angola (FNLA), the Union for the Total Liberation of Angola (UNITA) and the Popular Movement for the Liberation of Angola (MPLA). By March 1976 the MPLA had defeated its rivals thanks to Cuban troops (estimates of their numbers vary from 12,000 to 17,000) and Soviet military aid. In October 1976 Angola signed a treaty of Friendship and Co-operation with the Soviet Union. Angola also began aiding the South West Africa People's Organisation (SWAPO) guerrillas fighting to wrest control of Namibia from South Africa. Kissinger and Ford were concerned about this use of 'proxies' to extend Soviet influence. But Moscow felt they were responding to an American proxy, South Africa, which was backing UNITA. During the January 1976 visit to Moscow Brezhnev refused to discuss Angola. For Kissinger this was a test of US strength: failure to meet it might encourage further Soviet adventures. But Congress was in no mood to fund another Third World intervention. The Ford administration, however, was not willing to stop SALT II negotiations or the grain sales, though it regarded Angola as a worrying development. As Dunbabin says, 'The trouble was not that a Marxist government had come to power – this had been acceptable in Mozambique – but that it had been put there by open Soviet/Cuban intervention' [37: 322].

Conference on Security and Co-operation in Europe

If the Vietnam settlement had unravelled and US-Soviet tensions mounted over Angola, there was at least one success in East–West détente – the Helsinki Accords of August 1975. Multilateral Preparatory Talks for a Conference on Security and Co-operation in Europe (CSCE) took place in Helsinki from 22 November 1972 to 8 June 1973. The first formal sessions, known as stage I, were held in Helsinki from 3 to 7 July 1973. They were followed by meetings of the CSCE Coordinating Committee from 29 August to 3 September 1973 at Geneva. Stage II sessions, what one British diplomat called a 'long hard slog' were then held in Geneva from 18 September 1973 to 21 July 1975. In a meeting in Helsinki on 30 July to 1 August their recommendations were accepted by the leaders of thirty-five nations. The Helsinki Final Act, as this agreement was known, reached agreement on three broad areas known as baskets. In basket I they accepted the post-war European frontiers; and committed themselves to greater exchanges of military information. In basket II they promised fuller economic, scientific and technological co-operation. In basket III they pledged themselves to allow closer contacts between peoples and greater respect for human rights. The Soviet Union had wanted a European security conference to endorse their post-1945 position. They had achieved this but they had had to accept clauses on human rights that were to have unforeseen consequences. They provided a mechanism for criticism of Soviet rule by citizens of various Warsaw Pact states. Soviet refusal to countenance such criticism led to the repression of 'Charter 77' in Czechoslovakia and other such movements which, in turn, produced growing criticism of the Helsinki Accords and of détente in general.

The Decline of Détente

The domestic difficulties of the Nixon administration and the contest for influence in the Middle East and Africa had already put strains on détente before Ford became president. But attacks on détente increased after August 1974. Senator Henry Jackson argued that US-Soviet economic agreements should be tied to the Soviet performance on human rights. So Congress blocked the granting of Most Favoured Nation status to the USSR. Kissinger became the focus of criticism, leading Ford to remove him from the post of National Security Adviser in December 1975. The administration also stopped using the term 'détente'. During the 1976 presidential election détente was attacked from the Republican right by Ronald Reagan who claimed that Ford had negotiated away US nuclear superiority and legitimised Soviet dominance of Eastern Europe. Jimmy Carter, the Democratic candidate, charged the Ford and preceding Nixon administrations with lacking a moral dimension to its policy. He said he would pursue a foreign policy that stressed moral principles and human rights. If these American developments were damaging to détente, so too were Soviet interventions in areas of little importance to them likely to hinder co-operation.

Despite these pressures, attempts were still made to pursue détente. There was another round of multilateral talks, Mutual and Balanced Force Reductions (MBFR), which concerned conventional weapons. The Soviets had offered these talks so as to persuade the Europeans to participate in the CSCE. The Europeans were anxious about Congressional pressure to cut forces in Europe. So any conference that lessened the dangers through reductions by both sides was welcome. In May 1971 Brezhnev made a speech favouring cuts in forces in places, like Central Europe, where military confrontation was especially dangerous. In June 1971 NATO chose its Secretary-General, Manlio Brosio, to speak to the Soviets on this issue. In December 1971 NATO issued a ministerial communiqué declaring its readiness to see a European security conference and for there to be talks on MBFR. The May 1972 Nixon–Brezhnev summit finally agreed to move forward with both.

Preparatory discussions on MBFR were held in Vienna from January to June 1973. Formal discussions took place between 11 October 1973 and 16 December 1976. They failed to produce any concrete achievements. The failure was a result of the essential incompatibility of the two blocs' negotiating positions. Talks continued until 1989. Although no agreement was reached the British concluded that they had at least prevented any cuts in American forces in Europe and this had ensured that the Soviets had to maintain their own spending and this 'burden of unreduced military expenditure had made its contribution to the crippling of the Soviet economy' [35: 475]. Kissinger argued, 'We succeeded in keeping the issue of mutual force reductions alive to block unilateral American withdrawals by Congress; at the same time we succeeded in prolonging the negotiation without disadvantageous result' [68: 949].

Further progress on SALT was also stalled. November 1972 had seen SALT II talks formally begin. In November 1974 Ford and Brezhnev held a summit in Vladivostock where they agreed on a framework for SALT II. There would be an equal limit of 2400 missiles or bombers on each side with no more than 1320 of them with MIRV capability. The expectation was that the points unresolved at Vladivostock would be quickly settled and a treaty agreed. But negotiations were hindered by technical arguments about new weapons between the negotiators and by domestic criticisms within the United States. Kissinger's Moscow trip in January 1976 made advances but the Pentagon was critical [49: 596–599].

Conclusion

Nixon had entered office with grand plans. Many of them were realised. He successfully negotiated American departure from Vietnam. Diplomatic relations were established with communist China. Both Nixon and Kissinger initially resisted West German pursuit of *Ostpolitik* but it provided a significant prelude to American détente with the Soviet Union, resulting in the SALT I and ABM agreements and the Helsinki Accords. But domestic difficulties engulfed the administration: malpractices revealed by Watergate compelled Nixon's resignation. His successor, Gerald Ford, lacked the skills and vision but, most important, was restricted in his room for manoeuvre by a Congress suspicious of both the White House and of deals with Moscow. Both the new president and Brezhnev recognised that any new initiatives could not be pursued until after the presidential election in November.

6 The Demise of Détente and the New Cold War, 1977–1985

Jimmy Carter

James Earl (he preferred Jimmy) Carter defeated Gerald Ford in the 1976 presidential election largely because of a popular revulsion against the excesses of government in Washington. Watergate and claims about CIA involvement in Chile gave government an unsavoury image. Carter campaigned as an outsider who would restore morality to politics. An Evangelical Christian who promised 'I'll never lie to you', he had served for a term as Governor of Georgia but had no experience of Washington either as an elected politician or as an official. An honest, intelligent, knowledgeable, well meaning individual whose outlook was influenced by liberal and Christian ideals, he could become preoccupied with details and find it difficult to delegate. He never established effective relations with Congress. Garthoff feels he was naïve about bureaucratic and global politics. Worse, there were divisions among his advisers. Secretary of State Cyrus R. Vance and Secretary of Defense Harold Brown both possessed considerable experience in foreign and defence matters while Assistant for National Security Affairs Zbigniew Brzezinski brought a talent for conceptualising foreign policy ideas. However, they did not share a common outlook. Since Carter did not offer a sense of overall direction, the outcome was 'a policy that zigzagged' [49: 623].

Vance, a Yale educated lawyer, was pragmatic, polished and cautious, but shrewd and persistent. He shared the president's attachment to improving relations with less developed states.

123

Brzezinski was a tough, outspoken Polish immigrant who gained a PhD at Harvard and went on to be Director of Columbia University's Institute on Communist Affairs. While Vance favoured moving forward with SALT II, was wary of co-operating with China and sceptical about the alleged threat brought by Soviet intervention into Africa, Brzezinski was ready for closer ties with China and insistent on the need to resist Soviet moves in less developed regions. It was Brzezinski who won the competition for influence with the president. He had become Carter's mentor in international affairs in the mid-1970s when the former Governor of Georgia worked with the Trilateral Commission, formed to improve relations between the United States, Western Europe and Japan. Brzezinski became a full member of the cabinet, often chairing important meetings attended by Vance and Brown. Brzezinski came increasingly to influence Carter's outlook on relations with the Soviet Union. All members of the administration accepted that détente involved a mixture of co-operation and competition. According to Garthoff, Vance 'more often saw the possibilities' of co-operation', while Brzezinski 'more often saw the need for competition' [49: 624–625].

Yet Carter's foreign policy agenda involved a commitment to replace power politics with 'world order politics', which meant focusing on economic and social themes rather than on military force. He intended opening a dialogue between the rich and poor nations, paying more attention to human rights and trying to restrict the global arms race. In this latter case he was particularly sensitive to the US position as the world's leading arms supplier. He also sought to take the nation beyond the trauma of Vietnam and put the Soviet Union on the defensive [22; 33; 63].

An early indication that the administration would mark less of a departure than its rhetoric suggested came when, shortly after the election victory, a Carter aide, Hamilton Jordan, asserted, 'If after the inauguration you find Cy Vance as secretary of state and Zbigniew Brzezinski as head of national security, then I would say we have failed. And I'd quit... You're going to see new faces, new ideas'. Their subsequent appointments to these posts did not result in Jordan's resignation [102: 315].

According to John Lewis Gaddis, the Carter administration was attempting

> to do everything at once: achieve a breakthrough on SALT, implement a human rights campaign, deter Moscow from seeking incremental shifts in the balance of power, and at the same time move away from the excessive preoccupation with the Soviet Union that had characterized Kissinger's diplomacy. These were meritorious enough objectives, but they could not be attained at the same time: one could not simultaneously negotiate with, reform, deter and ignore the Soviet Union. [46: 350]

Carter's commitment to 'world order politics' lasted from about 1977 to 1979 without achieving any of its goals. The president's two successes – an agreement with Panama over the canal and brokering a treaty between Israel and Egypt – were the product of traditional diplomatic negotiations. In 1979 the president became notably tougher in response to the occupation of the US Embassy in Tehran by Iranian revolutionaries and adopted a strongly anti-Soviet outlook in reaction to the Soviet invasion of Afghanistan in December. He was encouraged to adopt this attitude by Brzezinski.

Successful Negotiations: Panama and the Middle East

Built in 1912, the Panama Canal was controlled by the United States who exercised sovereignty over a five-mile wide stretch of land on either side of the waterway. It was an important route for trade and for the US Navy. By the 1960s resentment at American control had grown. In 1965 there were demonstrations against the Americans. For the next ten years efforts were made to reach a deal with Panama. One was nearly achieved in 1975 but was not pursued after Ronald Reagan in the 1976 presidential election campaign accused President Ford and Kissinger of 'giving away our canal'. Carter, however, was determined to find a solution. In September 1977 his negotiators produced two treaties. The first gave legal control of the Canal Zone back to Panama after 31 December 1999;

until then, the United States would operate and defend the canal. The second neutralised the Zone and promised the United States the right to protect the 'neutrality of the waterway'. After initial hostility to the deal, the Carter administration launched a campaign to persuade the Senate and the public. It succeeded and on 16 March 1978 the Senate ratified the treaties [22: 152–185; 102; 120].

The Yom Kippur War had made the Arab–Israeli conflict an aspect of US-Soviet relations. It was probably Carter's greatest foreign policy achievement to find a partial amelioration of the problem. Kissinger had established a good deal of trust with a number of Arab leaders, in particular Anwar Sadat of Egypt. But he had not been able to achieve more than a military disengagement. Both Vance and Brzezinski sought to pursue a general settlement. Vance travelled to Israel and the Arab states. Carter hosted a visit by Yitzhak Rabin, the Israeli premier, but contrived to offend the Israelis by suggesting there should be a Palestinian 'homeland' and to upset Arabs by hinting that not all of the territory gained by Israel in 1967 would be returned. In April Carter met Sadat who had broken with the Soviet Union and was willing to see a greater US role in the search for a settlement. It seems he hoped that the Americans, pleased at Egypt's cutting of ties with the Soviets, might put some pressure on Israel. In May, however, Rabin was defeated in the Israeli general election by the hard line Menachem Begin. During his visit to Washington in July Begin said he would talk to the Arabs and consider leaving Sinai but wished to keep a foothold on the West Bank and refused to consider a Palestinian state.

It was Sadat who made the breakthrough. He told an American journalist, Walter Cronkite, that he was prepared to visit Israel. On 19 November he spoke to the Israeli Parliament, the Knesset, offering 'to live with you in permanent peace based on justice'. America now became involved as a mediator. Sadat came to the United States in February 1978, receiving a friendly reception from press, Congress and President Carter. Sadat told the Americans that he was ready to reach a bilateral agreement with Israel. Vance now tried to encourage a deal between the Israeli Foreign Minister, Moshe Dayan, and the Egyptian Foreign Minister, Ibrahim Khalil. But they failed to reach agreement at

Leeds Castle in Britain in July because the Israelis would not include a declaration of intent to quit all the occupied territories. So Carter decided to host a summit meeting between Sadat and Begin at Camp David. For two weeks in September Sadat, Begin, Carter and their aides argued over a 'framework' for peace. On Friday 15 September Carter said he would end the summit on Sunday night with or without a framework. This concentrated minds. Begin offered an ambiguous statement halting for a while any new Jewish settlements on the West Bank of the Jordan River; and agreed on an Israeli withdrawal from Sinai and the removal of Israeli settlements there. Sadat agreed to a separate peace treaty with Israel. Begin refused to include the issue of Palestine in the treaty, agreeing only to further conversations on the future of the West Bank. It required a further six months of pressure, cajolery and promises of aid from the Americans before Sadat, Begin and Carter signed the agreement on the White House lawn on 26 March 1979 [22: 273–403; 93].

The Horn of Africa: Ethiopia and Somalia, 1977–1978

While Carter had concentrated on Panama and the Egypt–Israeli agreement he had tried to pursue talks on SALT II but had presented proposals for lower levels of nuclear weapons than those agreed by Ford and Brezhnev at Vladivostock in November 1974. This irritated the Soviets. Yet they seemed oblivious to the provocative nature of their own actions. They became much more active in Asia, the Middle East and Africa. American concerns now focused on the Horn of Africa. There were, by February 1978, 15,000 Cuban troops in Ethiopia which was given about $1 billion of Soviet military assistance.

From the 1950s to 1974 the US had military facilities in Ethiopia. The Soviet Union backed the attempts at independence by Eritrea (an Ethiopian province on the Red Sea). It also formed an alliance with Somalia which became independent in 1960. It established a naval base at Berbera and in 1974 a Soviet–Somali Friendship Treaty was signed. In 1974 in Ethiopia the pro-Western Haile Selassie was overthrown and replaced by a military Dergue (junta). The new government developed closer ties with the Soviet Union, particularly after Colonel Mengistu

Haile Mariam became the dominant figure. This led the Americans in April 1977 to end their military assistance to Ethiopia. Then in July Somalia invaded Ethiopia to try and gain Ogaden which contained about a million Somalis. Moscow faced a quandary over which ally it should support. It decided to cut arms to Somalia, which now turned to America, cancelled its Friendship Treaty and expelled Eastern bloc advisers in November. The USSR sent arms, as well as transporting 15,000 Cubans and 1000 Soviet advisers to Ethiopia. This allowed the Ethiopians to repel the Somalians from January 1978 onwards. Opinion in Washington was divided on the meaning of Soviet intervention. For Vance and Brown this was not an important area, while Soviet policy appeared muddled. Brzezinski, however, asserted that the Soviets were challenging the US in an 'arc of crisis' from Africa across the Middle East to Central Asia. When Brzezinski said the Ogaden war would complicate SALT II talks, Dobrynin, the Soviet Ambassador in Washington, declared that Ethiopia would not advance into Somalia territory. This pledge was honoured in mid-1978 when Ethiopia regained all of the Ogaden and halted its forces [14; 120].

Although matters did not escalate, the Soviet intervention had worried the Americans. Their concerns were increased by further Soviet action. From 1977 onwards the Soviet Union began deploying its SS-20 intermediate-range nuclear missiles in Europe. As part of the Vladivostock accords Brezhnev had agreed to exclude the British and French nuclear weapons. To appease the Soviet military he had approved testing of new SS-20 missiles to replace the SS-4s and SS-5s. He also calculated that they might prove a useful bargaining counter when there was the possibility of the Americans developing Cruise missiles (low level radar-evading nuclear weapons). In early 1977 the Americans decided to proceed with their development. Shortly afterwards, Carter suggested revising the Vladivostock terms for SALT II talks. So the Soviets began deploying SS-20s in Europe. In response, the United States and NATO considered countering this by deploying their own intermediate-range missiles in Europe. Brzezinski also persuaded the president that America should play the 'China card' by establishing better relations with Beijing. Carter agreed.

China

Even after the February 1972 Beijing summit US-Chinese relations remained ideologically divided. There was continuing disagreement about Taiwan. The Watergate scandal and the defeat of South Vietnam troubled the Americans, while the death of Mao in September 1976 resulted in a power struggle in China. In addition, the progress of US-Soviet détente worried Beijing. But Carter wished to explore normalisation of relations. Cyrus Vance's talks in Beijing in August 1977, however, revealed the difficulties. The Chinese criticised SALT II and urged the Americans to adopt a firmer policy towards the Soviet Union. Vance himself also had reservations about doing anything to jeopardise Taiwan's security. The use of Cuban troops in Ethiopia, however, led Brzezinski to favour a tougher line towards Moscow and to recommend using the 'China card'. By 1978, then, both powers had reasons to reach a better understanding. China wanted access to American technology and expertise to help modernise the country and was worried about the Soviet alliance with Vietnam formed in November. The Americans were encountering domestic criticism of détente, while the Ogaden War brought public and Congressional condemnation of Soviet policy in the Third World. Brzezinski went to Beijing in May 1978 where he was less reticent than Vance had been about Soviet behaviour. He received an enthusiastic welcome and was able to set in train the process of normalising relations, which was agreed by December. It came into effect on 1 January 1979. In March they established embassies in their capitals [23]. This process was eased by cuts in US forces in South Korea in the late 1970s and by an agreement on Taiwan whereby the Americans ended their defence treaty and 'official' relations with Taiwan, and the Chinese undertook not to invade the island. The normalisation was confirmed by the first trip to the United States of a senior Chinese communist, Deng Xiaoping, in January–February 1979. Carter wrote in his diary about Deng, 'He's tough, small, frank, courageous, personable, self-assured, friendly, and it's a pleasure to negotiate with him' [22: 202].

Although the Carter administration continued its pursuit of SALT II, thereby irritating the Chinese, the normalisation was a step closer to China and a step away from the Soviet Union.

Unlike Nixon and Kissinger, Carter and Brzezinski did not try to exploit the Sino-Soviet split to play off the two countries against each other. Carter said 'everything went beautifully' in relations with China [22: 211]. Amity was not upset by Chinese military action against Vietnam. Although both were communist states, there were disputes between Vietnam and Kampuchea (as Cambodia was now known). Border skirmishes developed in 1977 into major conflict which escalated in 1978. After 1975 Soviet influence in Vietnam grew while China's waned. On 25 December 1978 Vietnam attacked Kampuchea. Then in February 1979 the Chinese launched a punitive assault on Vietnam partly to demonstrate their backing for Kampuchea and partly to assert their role in the region. Deng informed Carter of their intentions. The president argued against such action but did not press the point [22: 186–211; 120].

US-Soviet Relations and SALT II

Carter did not regard the improvement of US-Soviet relations as a priority. Rather, he wanted to give greater attention to relations with Western Europe and Japan and to the Third World. But he was interested in pursuing disarmament and arms control. So he wanted to see progress on SALT. To this end, he called, in January 1977, for a halt to nuclear weapons testing, and, over the next months, suggested various arms control talks. The SALT I treaty had left important loopholes that allowed the further development of nuclear weapons. Because it had excluded MIRVs, it was possible for both the Americans and Soviets, without violating SALT I, to augment their nuclear weaponry by introducing MIRVs which would increase the number of warheads. In addition, SALT I had only considered strategic weapons. The Soviet deployment of SS-20s in 1977 exposed these weaknesses of SALT I.

The Carter administration initially appeared likely to accept the Vladivostock terms for SALT II: each power could possess 2400 missiles or bombers with no more than 1320 of them having a MIRV capability. Certainly Vance wanted to do so. Brzezinski and Brown, however, aimed to improve Vladivostock through larger arms cuts. In a message to Brezhnev on 26 January and in a meeting with the Soviet Ambassador, Dobrynin, on

1 February 1977 Carter displayed his good intentions but also his naïveté when he proposed altering the Vladivostock formula and establishing lower ceilings for numbers of weapons. In March Vance visited Moscow and presented these proposals. As Garthoff says, 'It contradicted earlier signals to Moscow that the United States was ready to begin by consolidating the agreement "90 percent completed" by Ford and Kissinger in 1976'. The matter was not helped by being proposed in public and at such short notice. Moreover, the new proposal favoured the Americans. This was hardly a sound basis for a successful negotiation. Rather, as Garthoff observes, it made 'the Carter approach a new obstacle to American–Soviet relations' [49: 626].

The offer angered the Soviets who did not want to begin the SALT II talks anew. The Soviet Foreign Minister, Andrei Gromyko, told Vance during his trip to Moscow that his government was opposed to altering the Vladivostock accords, which had taken considerable effort to accomplish. The Soviets also said that a US-Soviet summit, initiated on an annual basis by Nixon and Brezhnev, could not be held unless SALT II was on the agenda. Eventually in September the Americans agreed to revert to the Vladivostock terms, with the proviso that more arms reductions would be included in a SALT III treaty. Carter found he had to pursue SALT II in the face of domestic criticism. Congress only approved the appointment of Paul Warnke as leader of the American delegation by a narrow margin in March 1978. Given Soviet intervention in Ethiopia, the president was urged to 'link' progress on SALT to the reduction of Soviet activities in the less developed regions. But Carter never really pressed such 'linkage'.

Carter assumed that he could maintain good relations with the Soviet Union and enlist it in deeper arms reductions, even while launching his crusade against human rights violations and for democratic values. But Moscow regarded Carter's approach to US-Soviet relations as both confusing and threatening. Brezhnev condemned Carter for contacting the Soviet dissident, Andrei Sakharov [49: 627; 46: 348].

Nevertheless, talks proceeded and by 9 May 1979 the text of a Final Treaty was released. It was signed at the only Carter–Brezhnev summit in Vienna on 15–18 June 1979. It was an improvement on the Vladivostock formula and on the tentative agreement reached by Kissinger in January 1976. There would be equal ceilings of 2400 strategic nuclear weapon launchers or heavy bombers which would fall to 2250 by 1985. No more than 1320 of these could be either MIRVs or air launched Cruise missiles. Up to 1200 launchers could be MIRVs. Up to 820 of these MIRVs could be on ICBMs. The agreement was to last until 1985. The Soviets ratified the treaty soon after the summit. The terms of the SALT II agreement were a significant improvement on its predecessor. They established numerical equality, restricted MIRVs and committed (but did not compel) the two powers to cut their missiles numbers by 1982.

But the Carter administration encountered difficulties from the Senate, many of whose members felt SALT II did nothing to halt what they saw as the trend towards growing Soviet military power. Concerns were expressed about larger Soviet missiles and the 'Backfire' bomber. There were also objections from outside Congress. A pressure group, Team B, challenged CIA estimates of Soviet military strength and succeeded in persuading the CIA to expand its calculations on Moscow's defence spending. The Committee on the Present Danger, which included figures from Team B, was revived in 1976 (it was originally formed in 1950 to press for increased military expenditure envisaged in NSC 68) to lobby against détente, especially SALT II. Its membership extended beyond the Republican right to include neo-conservatives, ex-liberals who felt the Democratic Party under-estimated the threat of communism. Some critics felt SALT II did not reduce nuclear weapons sufficiently, others wanted to link the treaty to the Soviet record on human rights. Although the Senate Foreign Relations Committee voted by nine votes to six in favour of ratification, SALT II was never ratified. Ratification was suspended after the Soviet invasion of Afghanistan in December 1979. In 1980, however, the two signatories agreed to abide by the terms of the treaty [22: 212–265; 49; 106; 112; 120]. Meanwhile, as the ratification process stretched out, events in Central Asia intervened.

Iran: The Fall of the Shah; American Hostages

On 11 February 1979 Islamic revolutionaries overthrew the Iranian monarchy and established a republic based on Islamic principles. It came as a surprise to the Americans. It ought not to have done so, for the revolution was the result of long-fermenting troubles. The revolution saw Iranian oil production cut by 90 per cent and the price of oil rise from $18 to $36 a barrel. Long queues for petrol at filling stations caused many in America to blame Carter. The crisis had an impact on thinking about American foreign policy, in particular attitudes to détente. There were 50,000 Americans working in the Shah's Iran – providing military training, building factories, operating oil fields. So the fall of the Shah and the deeply anti-American Islamic revolution added to doubts already being voiced about American foreign policy after the events in the Horn of Africa. When Carter allowed the Shah into the United States for treatment of his cancer of the spleen, the Iranian leader, Ayatollah Khomeini, condemned the Americans and encouraged his followers onto the streets. On 4 November 1979, while the SALT II ratification process dragged on, they attacked the US Embassy in Tehran, seizing fifty-six Americans. Fifty-two of these hostages were not released until January 1981, after a long series of negotiations and an abortive rescue attempt in April 1980. Carter toiled tirelessly in the final part of his presidency to secure their release. He persuaded Algeria to mediate a deal which brought their freedom in return for the unfreezing of Iranian assets in the United States. But, no doubt to humiliate Carter, the hostages were only freed once Carter had ceased to be president [15; 22].

There can be little doubt that the Iranian revolution hindered progress on détente. The assault on American prestige led to calls for more aggressive policies. This eventually resulted in the election of Ronald Reagan as president in 1980. In order to restore American credibility, he immediately began to build up the country's military forces even beyond the increases ordered by Carter.

Afghanistan

In this febrile mood the Americans interpreted the Soviet invasion of Afghanistan on 25 December 1979 as another threat to what they saw as a strategically important region. It is improbable, however, that Moscow was aiming to threaten Western access to oil. It is more likely that the military action was intended to obstruct the rise of another fundamentalist Islamic state on the Soviet frontier. In April 1978 the People's Democratic Party of Afghanistan (PDPA), a communist organisation, had seized power from President Daoud. The PDPA, however, found it difficult to reinforce its hold on Afghanistan because of its tendency to factional conflict. In March 1979 there was a four-day revolt in the city of Herat by a combination of Islamist guerrillas and various anti-communist groups. More than 5000 people died. The PDPA had asked for Soviet aid but Moscow had refused to help. The following months, however, witnessed growing Soviet assistance to the Afghan communists but opposition forces continued to attack government targets. Meanwhile the infighting among the PDPA did not abate. In October 1979 the deputy leader, Hafizullah Amin, assassinated President Nur Mohammed Taraki, the Soviet-supported communist leader. Moscow held an anguished debate about the situation, finally deciding to send its forces into Afghanistan on Christmas Day 1979 [14: 282].

It is likely that the Soviet intervention was the product of two defensive considerations. First, there was anxiety about the rise of fundamentalist Islam which could have disturbing consequences for Soviet control of its Central Asian Republics. Secondly, there was recognition of the need to support fellow communists, especially given Washington's support for the Islamist rebels. If the rebels were to win, would there be a move towards the West? Such considerations, when combined with the Carter administration's focus on human rights cases in the Eastern bloc and the Soviet Union, have led one study to suggest that 'what was at stake was ultimately the legitimacy of the Soviet regime' [14: 283].

The Americans, on the other hand, saw Soviet behaviour as offensive not defensive. Carter declared that the invasion amounted to a 'quantum leap in the nature of Soviet behaviour'. He withdrew the SALT II treaty from the Senate, halted the sale of US grain and high technology equipment to the Soviet Union and declared a boycott of the 1980 Moscow Olympics. He continued this new tough line in his State of the Union speech in January 1980. He enunciated what became known as the Carter Doctrine, which declared that, if any external power sought to secure control of the Persian Gulf, the United States would 'repel [it] by any means, including military force'. He also promised to raise defence spending by 5 per cent in real terms each year for the next five years [102: 332]. Unfortunately for Carter this new anti-Soviet line did not stop the erosion of public support for his administration.

Ronald Reagan and the 'Evil Empire'

In the presidential election of 1980 Ronald Reagan defeated Jimmy Carter. So the Carter presidency, despite its grand aspirations, ended with an intensified Cold War between the United States and the Soviet Union. The new president offered rhetoric that showed no sign that the tension would be lessened. Ronald Reagan won the presidency on a platform of a tougher America, one that would not reach deals that entrenched the power of the Soviet Union, which he was to call in 1983 the 'evil empire'. The new president embarked on a huge military buildup and a determined effort to roll back Soviet power through increased support and encouragement for anti-communist insurgencies around the world. By the close of his two terms of office, however, many of these promises had been changed, abandoned or over-taken by events. Having secured election by denouncing arms control and détente, Reagan ended up signing in 1987 one of the most far-reaching arms reduction agreements of the Cold War era. Having condemned the wickedness of the Kremlin, he developed in 1987 and 1988 a remarkable personal understanding with the Soviet leader, Mikhail Gorbachev, a relationship that was to contribute to the ending of the Cold War.

Ronald Reagan was born in Tampico, Illinois in 1911 and was educated at Eureka College. He worked for a period as a sports journalist on the radio before turning to acting in 1937, becoming a popular 'B-movie' actor. In 1947 he became president of the Screen Actors' Guild. He gave up acting and went into politics in 1964 by which time he had changed political allegiance from the Democrats to the Republics. He served two terms as Governor of California (1966–1974). He made three unsuccessful attempts to gain the Republican nomination for president in 1968, 1972 and 1976 before succeeding in 1980. Reagan possessed considerable personal charm and a remarkable talent for presenting his ideas to the public in a simple, direct way. He offered more than merely a performer's skill. He brought to his time in political office a vision centred on a few simple beliefs. He favoured minimising the scope of government and reducing taxation as much as possible. He was committed to opposing what he regarded as the evil of communism. As Mervin says, 'These guiding beliefs can be criticized for being excessively simplistic, but they gave the Reagan administration a clear sense of direction, an important quality that other administrations have lacked' [82: 217].

Despite the campaign rhetoric about strength and a sense of direction, American foreign policy under Reagan rarely demonstrated a coherent and consistent outlook. As Schulzinger says, 'Much of the difficulty was of the Reagan administration's own making. The White House staff warred with the heads of the departments of State and Defense, who often were at each other's throats as well' [102: 333]. There were six different occupants of the post of National Security Adviser. Two individuals served as Secretary of Defense, Caspar Weinberger (1981–1987) and Frank Carlucci (1987–1989). The first Secretary of State, Alexander Haig (1981–1982) encountered difficulties in establishing his influence. He later wrote, 'The necessity of speaking with one voice on foreign policy...never took hold among Reagan's advisers' [116: 350]. The second Secretary of State, George P. Shultz (1982–1989) was more successful, partly because he had better relations with the president but mainly because he won the battle for influence which the State Department had been waging with the NSC.

Tensions, 1981–1983

Once he assumed office Reagan embarked on a programme of increased defence expenditure, convinced that American power had declined relative to that of the Soviet Union. McMahon claims it had not done so [81: 146]. Reynolds, however, points out that, while SALT II gave the United States a 50 per cent advantage in strategic nuclear warheads, in 1974 the Americans had possessed a three to one advantage [96: 363]. Reagan set a five-year defence expenditure target of $1.6 trillion, which was $400 million above the increases that Carter had ordered. This amounted to the largest peacetime military buildup in US history. It included revival of the B-1 bomber, development of the B-2 Stealth bomber and of the Trident submarine missile system, enlarging the navy from 450 to 600 ships. For McMahon Reagan's policies amounted to 'a bid to re-establish US strategic superiority' [81: *146*]. This produced alarm among the Soviet leadership which became concerned that the Americans were trying to develop a first strike capability.

In addition, more funds were devoted to the CIA, in particular to expand its covert activities. The next few years saw US backing for anti-communist guerillas in Afghanistan, Angola and Cambodia. Central America was a particular target for this assistance. Reagan sent military advisers to El Salvador and they helped the country from succumbing to communist control. Extensive aid was sent to the Contras who opposed the Sandinista government in Nicaragua, which came to benefit from Soviet and Cuban help. The Reagan administration's efforts failed to secure a victory for the Contras. What was worse, in November 1986 support for the Contras became embroiled in scandal. It was revealed that Robert McFarlane, the National Security Adviser, had offered military parts to Iran, denied such equipment after the taking of US hostages, in return for help in releasing Americans abducted in Lebanon, and that the money for this was being secretly channelled to the Contras. An inquiry was critical of the administration's approach and of the NSC in particular – McFarlane's successor, John Poindexter resigned – but it did not find the president culpable.

Meanwhile, attempts were made to pursue arms talks. The SALT negotiations were now re-named by Reagan as the Strategic Arms Reductions Treaty (START) talks to convey his commitment to reductions and not just to limitations. There were also efforts to reach an understanding on the Intermediate Nuclear Forces (INF), namely SS-20s and Cruise missiles. In December 1979 NATO had formally decided to deploy Cruise and Pershing II missiles in Europe to counter the Soviet SS-20s. Responding to left-wing pressure especially in West Germany, NATO had also decided to hold further talks with the Soviets on arms control. These decisions became known as the 'dual track' approach. Moscow, however, showed no urgency to reach agreement. The decision to introduce Cruise and Pershing II missiles had only occurred after America's original counter to the SS-20s, the neutron bomb, was dropped by Carter in 1978. The Soviets had organised a very effective propaganda campaign against it in Western Europe. They hoped to achieve a similar success against the Cruise and Pershing missiles. They were encouraged in this hope by the resurgence of anti-nuclear protest movements in the early 1980s [96: 485–486]. The prospect of new nuclear weapons in Europe at a time when Washington was employing fierce anticommunist rhetoric produced anxiety in Western Europe expressed in demonstrations numbered in the tens of thousands. In October 1981 marches in London, Rome and Bonn each brought out over 250,000 people [81: 154].

Reagan also did not seem in any hurry to have arms talks with the Soviets. He subscribed to the view that conversations were best held when American strength had been restored: 'peace through strength' was his catchphrase. He was unwilling to hold talks with the Soviets until they were more conciliatory. Indeed, he did not meet Ambassador Dobrynin until February 1983, while the first discussions with the Foreign Minister, Andrei Gromyko, took place in September 1984.

The INF talks formally began in Geneva in November 1981. The atmosphere was immediately embittered by developments in Poland. The communist government of General Jaruzelski introduced martial law in December in order to suppress Solidarity, an independent, non-communist trade union that had emerged in 1980 and which, under the leadership of Lech Walesa, was becoming a significant political movement in Poland. Determined to avoid the collapse of the communist regime but chastened by its experience of intervention in Afghanistan, Moscow had pressurised Warsaw to take firm action. In any case, the two negotiating positions were far apart. The United States argued for a 'zero option' of no INF missiles while the Soviets claimed that there already existed an approximate parity that the new NATO deployment would disturb. By July 1982 the two teams at Geneva produced a provisional agreement: SS-20s would be limited to 75 and there would be 75 Cruise missiles but no Pershing missiles. Neither Moscow nor Washington decided to pursue this. Deadlock continued in both these conversations and the START talks which had begun in June 1982 [37: 181].

By 1983 US-Soviet relations had thus reached a low point. Soviet fears about the American arms buildup were heightened by Reagan's announcement on 23 March of the Strategic Defence

Initiative (SDI) programme, soon known as 'Star Wars'. Its aim was to establish a protective screen of lasers or particle beam weapons in space which would destroy any incoming nuclear missiles. Most scientific opinion regarded it as an expensive fantasy. But Reagan was honestly committed to it. He did not seem to recognise, however, that, if successful, Star Wars would undermine the Soviet nuclear deterrent and so greatly alarm the leadership in Moscow. In the same month Reagan only added to Soviet concerns when he made a speech in Orlando, Florida to Evangelical church leaders in which he called the Soviet Union an 'evil empire' whose days were numbered [94: 568–570].

Then in September 1983 a serious incident occurred. A Soviet fighter shot down a Korean Airlines flight, KAL 007, en route from Alaska to Seoul, South Korea, killing all 269 people on board. It had gone off course and entered Soviet air space and it seems probable that Soviet air defence mistook it for an American spy plane. The Reagan administration condemned the action in strong terms, calling it an 'act of barbarism', but Moscow was unapologetic. Though productive of sharp words, such an isolated event was not likely to lead to war. Yet it contributed to growing anxieties in Moscow. Yuri Andropov, who had become party leader after Brezhnev's death in November 1982, issued a special statement talking of the 'militarist course' being pursued by the United States [96: 488–489]. According to Oleg Gordievsky, who was working as a British double agent in the KGB, Andropov had believed since 1981 that the Americans were preparing for a nuclear war [9: 488, 501]. So, when the following month saw 7000 American troops invade the Caribbean island of Grenada, Moscow assumed this might be the beginning of a forward move by the West. The Americans intervened to overthrow a Marxist government that had seized power in a bloody coup, quickly defeating the 600-strong army and rescuing the almost 1000 Americans on the island. Reagan had feared another hostage crisis like the one in Iran.

The Soviets found even more aggressive intent in the NATO exercise 'Able Archer' in November 1983. It caused Moscow on 8–9 November to warn its missions abroad that American bases had been placed on alert [9: 503]. That same month witnessed the beginning of the deployment of Cruise and Pershing II missiles. Mrs Thatcher's re-election in Britain in May 1983 and the election of Helmut Kohl and the CDU in West Germany in March, who were both committed to accepting the American weapons, ensured that the Soviet peace campaign against the missiles would fail [96: 486–487].

The situation was complicated by changes in the Soviet leadership. The USSR was ruled by a succession of elderly men who were either too ill or too lacking in ability to develop effective policies. In November 1982 Brezhnev died. He was succeeded by Yuri Andropov, who had served as head of the KGB since 1967. Though a reformer, his ruthless suppression of dissidents endeared him to conservatives. He was an able individual but, unfortunately, he was a sick man. In February 1984 he died of liver failure. His successor, Konstantin Chernenko, was an individual of limited education whose impact was reduced further by suffering from emphysema. He died in March 1985.

The combination of tensions over Poland and flight KAL 007, opposition to Star Wars and anxieties about Grenada and the NATO manoeuvres, caused first Andropov, then Chernenko to develop a pessimistic view of East–West relations. In November 1983 the Soviets quit the INF talks and left the START discussions the next month. It was the first time in fifteen years that the Americans and Soviets were not even talking to one another.

Thaw, 1983–1985

Despite this seemingly more tense situation and the apparent prospect of confrontation, there were more encouraging signs. Shultz had always maintained that progress would have to await the arrival of the Cruise and Pershing II missiles. This would offer the position of strength from which Reagan might begin to negotiate. Such conversations might prove a vote winner in the 1984 presidential election. In any event, Gordievsky, who had now defected, was briefing the Reagan administration that the Soviets were genuinely fearful of an American attack. As Reagan wrote in his memoirs:

> Many people at the top of the Soviet hierarchy were genuinely afraid of America and the Americans. Perhaps this shouldn't have surprised me but it did ... Soviet officials feared us not

only as adversaries but as potential aggressors who might hurl
nuclear weapons at them in a first strike. [94: 588]

Given this, the president was keen to meet a senior Soviet leader
'in a room alone and try and convince him that we had no
designs on the Soviet Union' [94: 589]. To this end, he arranged
with Shultz the creation of a small group within the National
Security Planning Group with the task of opening new channels
with the Kremlin.

Reagan had always desired to hold conversations with
Moscow, though only when the American position was strong
and confident. He noted in his diary on 6 April 1984 that,
though some members of the NSC were hard line and against
any approach to the Soviets, 'I think I am hard line and will
never appease. But I do want to try to let them see there is a
better world if they'll show by *deed* they want to get along with
the free world' [94: 572]. According to McMahon, the Reagan
administration was also influenced by American domestic opinion.
The large-scale peace protests caused him to soften his rhetoric
in 1984 [81: 158].

An underrated influence in developments was the role played
by the Secretary of State, George Shultz. A talented man who
had been a professor of industrial relations before serving under
Nixon in a number of positions culminating in the post of Secretary
of Treasury, he brought astute judgment and a calm manner to
American diplomacy. More than any other figure in the administration, he favoured a more positive attitude to relations with the
Soviet Union. By 1984 Reagan was more receptive to this
perspective. In addition, as the Reagan presidency progressed,
Shultz won the bureaucratic battle with the hawks, in particular
Casper Weinberger, the Secretary of Defense, who was
succeeded in 1987 by Frank Carlucci, a more willing collaborator.
Moreover, after the Iran–Contra scandal in 1986, the NSC was
discredited.

In January 1984 Reagan gave a speech saying he was willing to
renew negotiations. In a section drafted by the president himself
he spoke of Jim and Sally and Ivan and Anya, two couples who
both longed for peace [81: 158–159]. On 24 September he
addressed the UN General Assembly and suggested a new framework for US-Soviet nuclear arms talks. He proposed that there

should be three sets of discussions, covering INF, START and, a new field, anti-satellite weapons (ASAT). On 28 September Reagan received Gromyko in Washington. The Soviet Foreign Minister was as 'hard as granite' in their 'three hours of give-and-take', unwilling to commit himself but giving the president the impression that the Soviets might return to discussions after the election [94: 605]. Following Reagan's election victory in November, the Soviets agreed to join talks under that framework [81: 159]. In a meeting with Shultz in January 1985 Gromyko agreed that these discussions should begin in March. That month, however, saw the death of yet another Soviet leader. Chernenko's successor would not be another ineffective and elderly figure. The party chose a younger, more dynamic leader – the fifty-four year old Mikhail Gorbachev.

Conclusion

The Carter presidency failed to deliver the promised improvements in superpower relations – partly because of the critical atmosphere and partly because of the limitations of the president. Reagan inherited the intensified Cold War of the Carter administration and seemed to promise even more confrontation. Yet there was always more to his outlook than this. By 1985 his insistence on US strength was still axiomatic but a willingness to pursue dialogue was more evident. The arrival of a new Soviet leader added a dramatic new element to US-Soviet relations. Gorbachev was to preside over, indeed was to contribute to, a fundamental shift in Soviet–American relations. The Cold War that had dominated the relationship between the two superpowers was about to be transformed.

7 Renewed Détente and the End of the Cold War, 1985–1991

Gorbachev

The appointment, in March 1985, of Mikhail Gorbachev as the new General Secretary of the Communist Party of the Soviet Union marked the beginning of a dramatic era in US-Soviet relations, although this was not immediately evident. Born in southern Russia in 1931, he is a man of high intelligence whose career had advanced under Brezhnev and Andropov. During the latter part of Chernenko's term of office Gorbachev had emerged as the dominant figure in the Politburo. He was an adept dissembler. In March 1985 he secured Gromyko's endorsement of his candidacy as General Secretary to succeed Chernenko. Yet four months later he would replace him as Foreign Minister. Gorbachev was not only younger and more vigorous than his immediate predecessors, he had a better, if limited, grasp of the West from his travels in Belgium, France, Italy and West Germany. He had established a reputation for action and he was going to need such a talent, given the condition of the Soviet Union in 1985.

Gorbachev was now leading a country with major problems. The war in Afghanistan was proving a costly failure. Sino-American relations were steadily improving. The Soviet system was extremely expensive – trade credits, aid and arms were costing between $15 billion and $20 billion annually after 1980 [110: 280]. There were systemic economic problems and growing dissident movements in Eastern Europe. By the beginning of the 1980s Soviet economic growth had fallen to zero. This was partly a function of low population growth – about

The Cold War, 1945–1991

1 per cent annually – and the burden of military spending in the arms race with the United States. Military expenditure amounted to one-sixth, perhaps one-quarter, of GDP. More important was the gross inefficiency of the Soviet command economy. A vast bureaucracy, which was a mixture of inefficiency, confusion and corruption, sought and failed to direct resources and manpower to produce goods and services. The result was an economy characterised by shortages and poor quality products. One way of keeping pace with the rapid growth of Western technology was for the KGB and other Eastern bloc intelligence services to find ways of acquiring this technology. The rise in oil prices in the 1970s obscured these problems for a while as the country benefited from higher prices for its Siberian oil. By 1975 the Soviet Union had become the world's largest oil producer. In the 1980s, however, prices began to decline [110: 281–283; 96: 540].

Added to these fundamental economic problems were social changes that made the population less submissive. The Brezhnev years had witnessed a shift in the balance of the people from the countryside to the towns and cities: in 1960 about 49 per cent of the Soviet population was identified as urban; by 1985 the percentage had risen to 65 per cent. There was also an increase in the same period in those with a university education from 2.7 per cent to 11 per cent. Khrushchev's building programme led to large numbers of people moving from communal flats to single-family apartments, an environment easier for discussion of politics. In addition, about 90 per cent of households now possessed television sets, which, though often unreliable, did offer a sense of the world beyond the USSR. Soviet difficulties were made worse by coinciding with considerable economic progress in the United States and Western Europe. Increases in international trade and the fall of commodity prices benefited the West, and saw the rise of the Asian 'Tiger' economies, while hurting the communist bloc countries. Technological change, in particular the revolution in computers and communications, left the Soviet bloc still further behind economically [96: 541–542].

Despite their seriousness, Gorbachev approached these problems with considerable optimism. He removed Brezhnev's cronies and created a team of like-minded individuals. He proved open to new suggestions from these figures but was clearly the leading exponent of the reforms favoured in this 'new thinking'. The new policies lacked detail but recognised that things needed to be changed, though he was careful, at first, to re-assure the conservatives. It should be emphasised that his proposals were designed to reorganise and revitalise the communist system, not to remove it, and to do so by reorganising the central government institutions. He aimed to improve the administration, to tackle alcoholism, to introduce computers and other high technology, and to do this using the traditional methods of the command economy. The outcome of his efforts was very limited. An event in 1986 helped crystallise his ideas about the needs for a more radical departure. In April 1986 there was an accident, due to the incompetence of the staff, at the nuclear power station near to Chernobyl in Ukraine. Gorbachev and his fellow reformers concluded that reform would have to be more fundamental if the country's problems were to be tackled. It would need more than just new, more energetic figures at the top. Too many people at all levels of the party apparatus were resistant to change, partly through self-interest, partly through ignorance. So he initiated a series of public debates to expose difficulties. The government would pursue *perestroika* (restructuring) and do this through *glasnost* (greater openness).

In July Gorbachev made his most important appointment when he replaced Gromyko (who was made President of the USSR) as Foreign Minister with Eduard Shevardnadze, First Secretary of the Communist Party in Georgia. Shevardnadze had no experience of foreign policy but he quickly adapted to his new role and came to play a vital part in Gorbachev's diplomacy. The American Secretary of State, George Shultz, later observed:

The contrast between him and Gromyko was breathtaking. He understood there was more to the world than the United States, the Soviet Union, and Europe. He could smile, engage, converse. He had an ability to persuade and to be persuaded. We were in a real diplomatic competition now – we couldn't [sic] just sit around and say that the Soviet positions were 'nothing new' or a 'catastrophe for the free world'. The Soviets were awake. We had to engage them. [100: 702]

Working with Shevardnadze, Gorbachev was equally optimistic about the prospects in international relations. Indeed, he had already impressed a most demanding cold warrior, Margaret Thatcher, the British Prime Minister. After meeting him in late 1984, she declared, 'I like Mr Gorbachev. We can do business together'. Even the SDI did not dispirit him. After all, the Soviets had always previously been able to copy American military technology. Although lacking in diplomatic experience, Gorbachev felt that personal contact with the American President might produce a breakthrough in Soviet–American relations. He was fortunate in the timing of his efforts. President Reagan, influenced by both his wife Nancy and by Margaret Thatcher, was showing a greater willingness to explore issues with Moscow.

The US Vice-President, George Bush, and Shultz met Gorbachev for the first time on 12 March during their visit to Moscow for Chernenko's funeral. He made an immediate impression on the Secretary of State. Although Gorbachev had extensive notes to hand, he soon put them to one side and began talking in global terms:

> He was articulate and spontaneous. He seemed to be thinking aloud... Gorbachev's free-flowing monologue showed a mind working at high intensity, even at the end of a long, hard day. He displayed a breadth of view and vigor, I thought, but his basic positions were ones we had heard before.

Shultz told Vice-President Bush that Gorbachev was an entirely different kind of Soviet leader. 'He was quicker, fresher, more engaging, and more wide ranging in his interests and knowledge. The content of our meeting was tough and his manner was aggressive, but the spirit was different. He was comfortable with himself and with others, joking with Gromyko in a way that emerged from genuine confidence in his base of knowledge and in his political abilities'. The Secretary of State was 'genuinely impressed with the quality of the thought, the intensity, and the intellectual energy of this new man on the scene' [100: 529–532].

It was fortuitous for US-Soviet relations that Gorbachev took office at a time when there were no major issues to overcome, such as Vietnam, Southern Africa after the Portuguese revolution of 1974, Ethiopia after the fall of Haile Selassie, and Afghanistan following the overthrow of Dauoud. The Reagan administration was worried that the Cold War might infect Central America after the revolution in Nicaragua in 1979 but the Soviets were now far less willing to intervene. Instead, as Dunbabin says, 'the contest largely took the form of rival defence build-ups and a publicity war (often justifying these build-ups by alarming portrayals of the other side's capabilities)' [37: 332]. Clearly this was partly due to each power choosing not push issues to crisis point. This highlights an important feature to Reagan's approach that is not always appreciated. Behind the rhetoric of a determination not to compromise in defeating the 'evil empire' Reagan was careful to keep communications open. He was encouraged in this direction by George Shultz, who served as Secretary of State from 1982. Reagan's attitude had already softened before Gorbachev's emergence: Americans were engaged after September 1984 in arranging talks with the Soviets, which began in March 1985 as Gorbachev assumed office [37: 183]. For all the propaganda, then, the situation by late 1984 was more propitious for dialogue than it might have seemed at the time.

Summits

Anxious to achieve a breathing space in foreign affairs to allow him to address the multiple domestic problems, Gorbachev began to make startling proposals that would permit him to seize the initiative in international affairs. In April 1985 he said he would place a temporary halt on the deployment of intermediate-range nuclear missiles in Europe and declared he would make this permanent if the Americans followed suit. This was hardly likely to be acceptable to the Americans because it would merely have frozen the Soviet advantage in these weapons. In August he announced a temporary moratorium on nuclear tests and invited the Americans to do the same. They declined partly because of the difficulty of verifying the other side's behaviour, but mainly because it would have halted work on SDI. Next, he sought a summit meeting with the American President. Vice-President Bush came to Chernenko's funeral in March 1985 with an invitation from the president for Gorbachev to meet him in Washington. The two sides debated a venue, before agreeing in May that it should be Geneva. In November 1985 Gorbachev and Reagan held courteous, even congenial fireside conversations in Geneva. They liked each other and a bond of trust began to emerge between them, but Reagan remained cautious. For all his reassurances to Gorbachev, he sanctioned the Defense Secretary, Casper Weinberger, to take a tough line towards the USSR. Relations between their wives, however, were not to prove so affable in this and later meetings. Gorbachev's translator has described an episode in December 1987 when Nancy Reagan was giving a tour of the White House to Raisa Gorbachev, who seemed determined to upstage the First Lady. Mrs Gorbachev had a PhD in philosophy and was used to leading discussions, while Mrs Reagan was a former Hollywood actress. Yet, though Raisa Gorbachev was a 'strong-willed woman', Nancy Reagan was 'positively iron-willed' [72: 104–105].

The failure of the November 1985 summit was followed by eleven months of extensive correspondence between Gorbachev and Reagan. It explored their ideas on disarmament in some detail; and was often punctuated by sharp disagreements over issues like Afghanistan, Nicaragua and human rights. In 1986, however, Gorbachev decided to make concessions. He intimated that the Soviets would no longer link Soviet SS-20s to British and French nuclear weapons. A further summit was held in October 1986 in Reykjavik. The two leaders deepened their mutual understanding and even came close to reaching agreement to remove all ballistic missiles. The stumbling block, however, was Reagan's continued commitment to SDI [94: 642–679].

Mrs Thatcher was concerned about the possible elimination of strategic nuclear missiles, for she regarded them as one of the foundations of peace after 1945. She therefore sought to encourage Gorbachev and Reagan to concentrate on securing a deal on the intermediate-range weapons. By September 1987 the American and Soviet Foreign Ministers were able to announce that they had reached an INF agreement removing all intermediate-range weapons from Europe, the so-called 'zero option'. Although Gorbachev tried to tie the deal to SDI, he did not push the link when the Americans resolutely refused. Gorbachev chose not to press the matter on Star Wars because his advisers maintained that the US Congress would control SDI for him. Indeed this happened. Three weeks before the December 1987 Washington summit Congress cut the SDI budget by a third. So, at the Washington summit in December 1987 Gorbachev and Reagan signed one of the most significant arms treaties of the twentieth century. It involved the verified destruction of all ground-launched nuclear missiles with a range of 500–5500 kilometres in Europe and Asia. The INF Treaty, quickly ratified by the US Senate, saw the destruction of 1846 Soviet nuclear weapons and 846 US weapons in the next three years. This was verified through careful inspection of each side's nuclear sites, an unprecedented concession. 'For the first time in the atomic era, an entire class of nuclear weapons was being not just limited but eliminated' [81: 163]. The scale of the achievement fostered public enthusiasm, which was heightened by the hitherto unprecedented sight of the Soviet leader and his wife mingling with the American public.

Shultz wrote in his memoirs:

> The results were a tribute to the persistent effort of Ronald Reagan to stick to his basic objectives, to maintain our strength and the cohesion of our alliances, and to be willing to recognise an opportunity for a good deal and a changed situation when he saw one. President Reagan had the courage of his conviction that Gorbachev represented a powerful drive for a different Soviet Union in its foreign policy and in its conduct of affairs at home. Mikhail Gorbachev had come into power in 1985 with a difficult set of problems. He was perceptive enough to see them and bold enough to be decisive in dealing with the critical foreign policy issues that we faced. I admired and respected both leaders, and I had told them so. [100: 1015]

He might have added his own contribution. Oberdorfer describes Shultz's role as being of 'central importance in Washington, given the paradoxes in Reagan's views and the endless disputes within his administration until its final year. Reagan knew that he wanted a less dangerous relationship with the Soviet Union, but he did not know how to go about achieving it'. Shultz contributed two vital ingredients: the persistent pursuit of improved relations through the achievement of practical goals, like arms agreements and understandings on regional conflicts; and the organisational expertise to galvanise 'at least parts of the fractious US government'. 'Reagan wanted it to happen; Shultz was the key figure in his administration who made it happen'. 'Shultz was undeterred by the many obstacles, disappointments, and setbacks along the way. Like the tortoise in the race with the hare, he just kept coming, moving slowly but relentlessly toward the gaol' [87: 480]. Shultz and Shevardnadze also developed an effective partnership. Korchilov records a characteristic exchange at the December 1987 summit. Shultz made his speech about the need to proceed openly. At the close of his remarks he came to shake Shevardnadze's hand: 'They briefly stood there in the spotlight, like two old friends. It was one of the most emotional and memorable moments at lunch, provoking a long round of enthusiastic applause'. Gorbachev then delivered a speech praising the efforts of Shultz and Shevardnadze in making the INF treaty possible [72: 109–110].

There was also progress on other sources of Soviet–American friction. In 1979 Gorbachev had felt that the invasion of Afghanistan was a 'fatal error'. At the 1985 summit he suggested that Soviet withdrawal might be part of a wider US-Soviet settlement. By the 1987 summit he declared that the Soviets would quit. In April 1988 he agreed to remove Soviet troops, which was accomplished by February 1989. It was a remarkable decision by Gorbachev, given that it might involve the fall of a communist government in Afghanistan. The Afghan government survived until 1992, longer than the Soviet Union.

Indeed, this was part of a general Soviet withdrawal from the less developed world. Involvement directly in Afghanistan or indirectly through the Cubans in Angola and Nicaragua and the Vietnamese in Cambodia, was extremely costly – Cuba received $4 billion and Vietnam received $1 billion annually [110: 280]. South Africa occupied Namibia, even though the UN had ended its mandate; and it would not recognise SWAPO as the legitimate representatives of Namibians. The South Africans also supported UNITA in its fight against the Angolan government. Some 40,000 Cubans aided Angola and SWAPO assaults in Namibia. American assistance (Reagan viewed the dispute in Cold War terms) to UNITA helped them in their fight. It is probable, however, that Gorbachev's decision in 1987 to seek a settlement was more significant in solving the problem. The result was a US-Soviet deal in May 1988 involving Cuban withdrawal from

Angola and Namibian independence. The departure of the Soviet-sponsored Vietnamese from Cambodia was also the consequence of a decision by Gorbachev in 1987: it was a protracted affair, taking until 1991 [120: 592–594]. There was also progress on Sino-Soviet tensions. In a July 1986 speech Gorbachev recognised the border as the middle of the river and not the Chinese bank. This ended the bloody conflict that had occurred since 1969 over the islands in the middle of the river. He also announced the withdrawal of 10,000 Soviet troops from Mongolia. In May 1989 he became the first Soviet leader to visit Beijing since Khrushchev in 1950s.

At the May–June 1988 Gorbachev–Reagan summit in Moscow both leaders pursued the possibility of a 50 per cent cut in strategic nuclear missiles. In his memoirs Reagan says he had hoped to sign a START agreement at this meeting. Experts from both countries had been working on the matter since spring but had failed to resolve a number of questions, especially over sea- and air-launched cruise missiles. They told the president that they expected to solve these issues but not before he left office [94: 705]. When the American president raised concerns about human rights and religious freedom Gorbachev did not bristle as he had done at previous meetings. Moreover, Reagan gave an address at Moscow State University on what he called the 'blessings of democracy and individual freedom and free enterprise' [94: 713–714].

The last months of the Reagan presidency might not have seen a START agreement but they saw further progress in lessening tensions. Between 1985 and 1987 Gorbachev had increased defence spending but he then froze it and set about turning the military from its traditional offensive outlook towards his new notion of 'reasonable sufficiency'. In 1988 he proposed a pan-European disarmament summit. Gorbachev spoke to the UN on 7 December 1988 and said that the world was becoming less ideological and that 'force and the threat of force can no longer be...instruments of foreign policy'. He then announced large-scale reductions in Soviet conventional forces. There would be a cut of 500,000 men and significant withdrawals from Eastern Europe. These were to be a prelude to the aim of halving strategic nuclear weapons in the START talks. NATO responded by suggesting East–West reductions to a common ceiling (thus eliminating the Warsaw Pact superiority that it put at three to one in tanks). In early 1989 the useless MBFR talks were replaced by geographically less restricted ones, and in May the Warsaw Pact agreed to common ceilings in central Europe [37; 94; 110; 120].

1989

There are various claims as to when the Cold War came to an end. Mikhail Gorbachev, Margaret Thatcher and George Shultz all felt that this had been accomplished by the end of 1988. They justified this by pointing out that East–West tensions were significantly reduced, Moscow now respected human rights, and there was stabilisation and reduction in the deployment of nuclear weapons. Moreover, Gorbachev had announced cuts in conventional forces and said that ideology should not drive foreign policy. Yet in early 1989 Germany was still divided, there were communist regimes in Eastern Europe, and NATO and Warsaw Pact forces, numbered in the hundreds of thousands, faced one another in Central Europe. There were still two rival political systems in Europe.

A new American president confronted these circumstances. After Reagan completed his two terms, his Vice-President, George Bush, won the November 1988 election, defeating Michael Dukakis, the Democratic Party's candidate. Bush came from a rich New England family, had served as Navy pilot in the Pacific during the Second World War, and had completed a degree at Yale University prior to working in the oil industry for a decade. He then turned to government service, acting as US Ambassador to the UN, emissary to China, and director of the CIA before serving as Reagan's Vice-President for eight years. He therefore brought considerable experience of government and of foreign policy. A reticent, undemonstrative and decent individual, he listened rather more than he spoke. His approach was to talk directly to key figures in the administration outlining the central tenets he wished to pursue. He established a team of like-minded individuals, people who shared 'his penchant for low-key rhetoric and careful attention to details and the conse-quences of actions' [121: 20–21]. He was not the cold blooded and uncaring patrician of many a portrait of him. He regarded personal relationships as more important than political ideas. This lack of interest in ideas led to the claim that he lacked a vision for his presidency. Unlike Reagan, he was not driven by an urge to change the world. For Bush a president did not need a blueprint. Integrity, knowledge, a sense of public duty and experience were the essential requisites for office [83: 21–22].

James Baker was appointed as Secretary of State. He and Bush had been close friends for over a quarter of a century. Born in Texas to a prominent family, Baker was educated at Princeton, had qualified as a lawyer and had served in the Marines. He had worked in Washington in a number posts since the 1970s. He acted as White House Chief of Staff and then as Secretary of the Treasury under Reagan. The Texas drawl masked a man of some intensity, who knew how to cut to the heart of an issue and was always focused on how to solve the problem [121: 21–22]. Bush and Baker not only shared a personal friendship of long standing. They had similar political outlooks. Like his chief, Baker was not attracted to ideas. He was a pragmatist. Although a man of limited experience in foreign affairs, he had a sound grasp of bureaucratic politics in Washington. Indeed, he brought his own team of advisers with him to avoid becoming the captive of the State Department professionals. This undoubtedly caused some resentment among officials. Moreover, it might have guaranteed that he retained control of policy making but it also meant there would be missed opportunities [83: 160–162].

Dick Cheney, a Congressman from Wyoming who had served as Chief of Staff to President Ford, was appointed as Secretary of Defense. He brought to his post a straight-talking style and good relations with members of both parties in Congress. The knowledgeable, experienced and self-effacing Brent Scowcroft became National Security Adviser. He avoided, as he had done when he had served in the post for President Ford, becoming a rival to the Secretary of State in shaping foreign policy. He regarded his function as offering options to the president rather than being the initiator of a grand strategy. Baker, Cheney and Scowcroft formed an effective and harmonious team, far removed from the squabbles between the president's advisers in the Reagan administration.

The Soviet Union still dominated Eastern Europe in 1989. Poland was the first country to test Soviet control. Pressure came from Solidarity, the independent trade union turned political movement. This produced, on 6 February, round table talks that led to an agreement in early April that there would be partly free elections involving not just the Communist Party. The June elections brought a massive victory for Solidarity. August and September were months of crisis, as Moscow had to decide whether to allow a non-communist government. Eventually, a compromise was reached. There would be a non-communist premier but the posts of defence minister and interior minister would be held by communists. In September Tadeusz Mazowiecki became the first non-communist prime minister in East-Central Europe since 1948. The dominance of the communists was removed but Moscow did nothing. Instead, Gorbachev's press spokesman, Gennady Gerasimov, announced what he called the 'Frank Sinatra Doctrine': they could all 'do it their way'. Meanwhile, in Hungary the government allowed the people, on 16 June, to honour the hero of the 1956 uprising, Imre Nagy, thereby permitting the expression of a considerable amount of nationalist feeling. The Hungarian government also opened its border with Austria in May. This led to a huge influx of East Germans who used this as a route to the West. As this traffic mounted in July and August the GDR demanded that it be halted. When the Hungarians restricted the movements across their borders, the East Germans began arriving in huge numbers at the West German embassies in Budapest and Prague. This reached crisis point in August but a deal was struck allowing these refugees to travel to the West on trains that passed through East Germany.

The crisis facing East Germany deepened at the very time when its status should have been celebrated. Gorbachev came to the GDR in October for the fortieth anniversary of the creation of the state. The warm welcome he received, his coolness towards Erich Honecker, the East German leader, and the series of demonstrations in favour of reform across the country – all signalled a major crisis for the communist authorities. They faced a clear choice. Should they follow the example of the Chinese communists? The latter had encountered a movement for reform and a huge demonstration in Tiananmen Square in Beijing and had decided in June to suppress it violently. The GDR certainly had the ability to impose a 'Chinese solution' but those arguing for reform won the debate because they were supported by Moscow. 'The ruling party's will was undermined by self-doubt and widespread internal frustration with the stagnant leadership headed by Honecker' [121: 82]. It would appear that Gorbachev thought that the best way of saving East Germany was to initiate *perestroika*-style reforms. A new leader, Egon Krenz, took office with this goal. More demands were made, including the right to freedom of travel. In granting this, the authorities made a bureaucratic error by not excluding Berlin (normally given special status). Gunter Schabowski, the GDR spokesman, then compounded the mistake. The new regulations were due to come into effect immediately after the East German legislature had approved them. But Schabowski said they would apply immediately. This produced a clamour by thousands of people at the Berlin wall. The border guards were without instructions and did not know what to do. Under pressure from the crowds and reluctant to use force, they gave way and opened the wall on the night of 8–9 November and almost immediately people began to tear it down [121: 81–99].

November 1989 also saw changes in Czechoslovakia – the so-called 'Velvet Revolution'. Demonstrations organised by the newly created 'Civic Forum', the brainchild of the celebrated playwright, Vaclav Havel, led to the collapse of the government. On 29 December the Czech Parliament chose Havel as president. Also in December Romania witnessed its own 'refolution', a word coined by Timothy Garton Ash to convey the sense that the changes amounted to more than reform but were too orderly to be regarded as a revolution. This time the fall of the regime brought bloodshed: President Ceausescu and his wife were executed. A National Salvation Front had acted as the vanguard of action and then won the June 1990 elections.

In the space of a few months five states had witnessed the collapse of their pro-Soviet communist regimes. Poland, Hungary, East Germany, Czechoslovakia, and Romania were then joined by Bulgaria in the middle of 1990. This was achieved, in the main, by peaceful means. In essence, unpopular, economically inefficient governments collapsed under the weight of popular protest when Gorbachev made it clear that he would not apply the Brezhnev Doctrine, which involved armed intervention to maintain the communists' control of power. The costs of Soviet aid to these regimes was proving prohibitive for the Soviet Union – in

1981, it is estimated, the subsidy to Poland alone cost $1 billion. The nature of the American response no doubt helped. The CIA Director, Robert Gates, has written, 'He [Bush] did not gloat. He did not make grandiose announcements. He did not declare victory' [120; 37]. The Gorbachev–Bush summit in Malta in December 1989 confirmed the new spirit of co-operation. It also witnessed the end of the clash of two economic systems, for the Soviets accepted aid on condition that they improved human rights and moved towards a market economy. The transformation was staggering. As one historian notes, 'The Americans now regarded the USSR as an ally in eastern-central Europe… Ideology, mistrust, historical analogies and the other forces that had produced the Cold War antagonism were replaced by co-operation between Western and Soviet leaders' [99: 138].

German Reunification

The reunification of Germany was achieved within a year of the fall of the wall and has led many to assume this was an inevitable process. It was no such thing. Chancellor Helmut Kohl of West Germany and the Bush administration pursued German unity. The Soviet Union, Britain and France all had their reservations. Thatcher and François Mitterand, the French President, were wary of the power of a united Germany. Gorbachev had decided that Soviet security no longer required the East European satellite states. Germany was different. It had been at the centre of Soviet defence strategy since 1945. Moreover, as Shevardnadze said, 'We had paid an enormous price for it and to write it off was inconceivable. The memory of the war was stronger than the new concepts about the limits of security' [81: 166]. But the West Germans and Americans outmanoeuvred them.

No sooner had the wall come down than Kohl began pressing for reunification. Opinion polls in West Germany indicated its popularity and the signs of collapse in the GDR suggested little opposition there. Bush readily agreed, believing the division of Europe could be ended on Western terms. Meantime the East German state was disintegrating. In December 1989 Krenz resigned and Hans Modrow became leader. He now agreed to multi-party elections for March 1990. By January 1990 Gorbachev had decided to concede German reunification. There were three reasons for his decision: the collapse of the GDR, Soviet economic troubles and a desire to build co-operation with the West. So in February Kohl announced talks on economic and monetary union with East Germany. In the same month the Americans suggested that the issue of a unified Germany be pursued in what came to be known as 'two plus four' talks. The two Germanys would address the domestic issues while the four occupying powers, Britain, France, the Soviet Union and the United States, would tackle the international questions. This proposal was accepted in an unprecedented joint meeting between NATO and the Warsaw Pact later in the month. Kohl then visited Moscow and concluded a deal that granted economic assistance to the Soviet Union. The East German elections in March returned a vote of 48 per cent for Kohl's CDU candidates, while the socialists (SPD) gained 22 per cent and the communists secured 16 per cent. The new government agreed to join West Germany.

On 14 March 1990 'two plus four' talks began between officials. A major issue concerned whether the new united Germany would remain a member of NATO. By the time of the first minis-terial meeting in May the misgivings about a united Germany felt by Mitterand and Thatcher had subsided. Kohl's offers of financial assistance to Moscow to cover the costs of the departure of Soviet forces and of limits on the size of the German army softened Gorbachev's objections to Germany remaining in NATO. In his summit meeting with Bush in May he was reassured. Meanwhile, Kohl forced the pace. In July there was economic and monetary union of the two Germanys. A few days later there was a meeting between Kohl and Gorbachev. They agreed that the German army would be limited to 370,000, Germany would accept its existing borders, there would be financial aid for the Soviet withdrawal (this eventually amounted to $9.5 billion), a Soviet–German Friendship Treaty would be signed, Germany would be a full member of NATO, and Soviet occupation rights would end. The Final Settlement on Germany was agreed in September 1990. It accepted the Kohl–Gorbachev accords: the four occupying powers surrendered their rights in Germany. All-German elections were held in December and produced a

CDU victory: they gathered 46 per cent to the SPD's 33 per cent and the communists' 10 per cent [121; 21; 12].

German unity had come as a result of Kohl's exploitation of East Germany's collapse. He had received the sympathetic support of the Bush administration. Gorbachev's readiness to accept a unified Germany was partly the product of the logic of his own 'new thinking'. He could hardly argue against the clear wishes of the German population after saying that he favoured allowing countries to go their own way. More important was what was happening in the Soviet Union. The growing economic problems made the offers of West German financial aid especially appealing. Shevardnadze was bitterly attacked in Russia for the Soviet decision to permit German unification. He resigned in December 1990.

German reunification coincided with another major disarmament agreement. The Conventional Forces in Europe (CFE) Treaty was signed in November. The MBFR talks were renamed the CFE discussions in January 1989 and negotiations began in March. By the time the thirty-four nations gathered in Paris agreement had been reached. This would apply to military equipment rather than numbers of troops. Each alliance would be allowed a total of 20,000 tanks, no more than 13,300 of them belonging to one country. The meeting also produced the Charter of Paris, a declaration of democratic rights and individual freedoms.

Events in 1990 constituted a watershed. If 1989 saw the end of the ideological struggle between East and West and the collapse of communist rule in Eastern Europe, then 1990 marked the decisive, irrevocable shift by removing Germany as an issue. Disagreements about Germany, after all, had precipitated the US-Soviet division. McMahon is surely right to argue that the reunification of Germany marked the end of the Cold War [81: 166]. The Kremlin was now preoccupied with the internal disintegration of the USSR

Collapse of the Soviet Union

The unification of Germany and the CFE Treaty helped to accelerate the crisis of authority in the Soviet Union. Gorbachev's policies had unleashed forces for change not only in Eastern Europe but also within the Soviet Union. Indeed, the nationalists in the USSR were encouraged by the revolutions in Eastern Europe. From the beginning of his leadership Gorbachev spoke about the need for the democratisation of Soviet society. It was not until the summer of 1988 that he moved from liberalisation to democratisation. He now accepted the principle of contested elections for a new legislature. By this time his policy of *glasnost* had broken down taboos and encouraged greater political debate. The March 1989 elections saw the defeat of a number of Communist Party functionaries and brought into the legislature nationalists from Baltic and Caucasian republics as well as a number of Russian liberals and radicals. Gorbachev found himself under pressure from radicals like Boris Yeltsin, and from defenders of the communist system within the party and state apparatus, including the military and KGB, who feared the effects of such far-reaching changes. By late 1990 he had backed away from his more radical economic policies and started to court the conservatives. In December 1990 Shevardnadze resigned as unrest grew within the USSR.

The decisive test of the limits to Soviet coercion came in the Baltic republics, especially Lithuania. In August–September 1989 Lithuania became engulfed by mass popular protests and elected nationalist leaders. In March 1990 they declared themselves independent. A violent Soviet response was only averted by the Lithuanians deciding to suspend their declaration. There was also pressure for full independence in Ukraine, Georgia and Armenia. The most surprising advocate of independence, however, was the Russian republic. Yeltsin had been elected to the People's Deputies of the USSR in 1989 and in May 1990 had been appointed President of the Russian Republic, which was to be endorsed in direct elections in June 1991. In his desire for power, Yeltsin in August 1990 argued that Russian laws had supremacy over Soviet law.

In January 1991 the government began a violent crackdown in Lithuania. But Gorbachev equivocated as he faced pressure from hardliners to re-assert Soviet control and from foreign countries and the remaining reformers in Moscow to find a peaceful solution. He wanted to avoid bloodshed and mass protests and so developed the idea of a 'Union of Sovereign States' to replace the USSR. It would extend substantial autonomy to the local republics. This, however, was a step too far for the hard-liners. The KGB chief, Vladimir Krychkov, and his allies, the premier, Valentin Pavlov, the head of Soviet military industry, Oleg Baklanov, and Minister of Defence, Dmitry Yazov, tried to seize power in August 1991. The focus of opposition to the coup was the Russian 'White House', home of the Russian parliament, where Boris Yeltsin, now president of the Russian republic, rallied tens of thousands of Muscovites who surrounded the building. The coup therefore failed when the majority of the security forces refused to assault the 'White House'. When Gorbachev returned to Moscow he was the leader of a shell state. Power now lay with the leaders of the various republics with Yeltsin the most powerful. On 8 December 1991 the presidents of Russia, Ukraine and Belorussia (Belarus) announced unilaterally that the USSR was dissolving and would be replaced by a Commonwealth of Independent States (CIS). On 21 December all the other republics, except the Baltics and Georgia, adhered to the CIS. Recognising reality, Gorbachev resigned on 25 December. The Soviet Union had ceased to exist. At least these last months of the Soviet Union brought the July 1991 START agreement in which Washington and Moscow pledged to halve their nuclear warheads to about 6000 by 1998.

Conclusion: Why the Cold War Ended

The Cold War was, in essence, an ideological struggle between communism and liberal democracies with market economies as well as a geopolitical competition between the Soviet Union and the United States and their allies. Given that communism collapsed in Eastern Europe and the Soviet state disintegrated while free market economies prospered and expanded and the United States grew stronger politically, economically and militarily, one might conclude that the Cold War had resulted in a victory for the West. Some writers challenge such a black and white verdict. Richard Ned Lebow's view is encapsulated in the title of his book, *We All Lost the Cold War*.

So why did events unfold as they did? Many say that it was due to Ronald Reagan who put pressure on the Soviet economy by increasing US defence expenditure to such a level that the USSR could not compete and so sought reductions to lessen their military costs and was willing to consider political reforms that would reassure the Americans sufficiently for them to cut back their own military forces. Such records as we have of the Reagan presidency do not indicate any conscious effort by the administration to pursue such a policy. Even though this was not what was intended, did this sequence of interreactions nevertheless cause the end of the Cold War?

Other writers, such as Robert McMahon, suggest that Gorbachev's arrival as Soviet leader in March 1985, not Reagan's policies, was the decisive ingredient. He brought a fresh approach to Soviet policy that involved a willingness to engage in serious dialogue with the United States. He made the vital concessions that led to arms agreements; for example, he dropped his opposition to SDI and so made it possible to achieve the INF Treaty. He abandoned the Brezhnev Doctrine of armed intervention to sustain communist rule and so allowed or, at least, did nothing to halt, the rise of protest which led to the fall of the communist regimes. Gorbachev changed policies in order to ease pressures on the Soviet Union. He was the first Soviet leader to acknowledge the full scale of the country's economic difficulties. He knew that these could only be tackled by reducing the massive defence spending burden and by reforming economic practices. Achieving these goals required an easing of the Cold War to justify a smaller, less costly military and better relations with the West that allowed the technology transfers and various commercial deals needed to help the Soviet economy. Clearly these policies were the result of Gorbachev's decisions. They were not a forgone conclusion. Other options were advocated within the Kremlin but Gorbachev was able to reject them because he possessed the political skills to secure the backing of the Politburo in Moscow and to win support in the West.

Although the case for Gorbachev's crucial role is very persuasive, it begs the question why he and the new generation of like-minded reformers came to believe they had to follow this course of action. The essential answer lies in the failure of the Soviet system. By the 1980s the accumulated problems of more than sixty years had produced enormous economic problems. What made it especially bad was that these surfaced at a time when the US economy was leaping forward thanks to what some dubbed another industrial revolution with the emergence of computer technology and the arrival of the 'information age'.

But what led Gorbachev to make the vital concessions? Because he concluded that this was the only way of coping with the pressure he was confronting. And these pressures were not only the legacy of history, the years of worsening problems left unaddressed. Reagan's policies, whether consciously or not, intensified them. As Sewell says, the Americans drove hard bargains [99: 131]. The INF talks were close to failing in 1987. Gorbachev at first did not want to make all these concessions. But, by stages, he came to see that the changes he wanted for the Soviet Union would not be possible without them. Reagan proved surprisingly adept in responding to circumstances. The American president seized the moment, saw the direction of Gorbachev's policy and encouraged it. As Gaddis makes clear, 'the President had a decisive impact on the course of events' in a number of ways: his support for SDI which unsettled the Russians;

> endorsement of the 'zero option' in the INF talks and real reductions in START; the rapidity with which the President entered into, and thereby legitimised, serious negotiations with Gorbachev once he came into office; and, most remarkably of all, his eagerness to contemplate alternatives to the nuclear arms race in a way no previous president had been willing to do.

He adds that Reagan recognised that his approach of 'nego-tiation from strength' was the 'means of constructing a domestic political base without which agreements with the Russians would almost certainly have foundered' [47: 131]. So, if Gorbachev took the decisive steps, they were forced on him by the legacy of history and by Reagan's general approach and the negotiating acumen of his foreign policy team led by Shultz.

Conclusion

A number of factors were responsible for the Cold War: the ideological differences between the Soviet Union and the West, the nuclear arms race, misperceptions of each other's intentions and the overestimation of each other's capabilities. Initial American post-Second World War plans did not go much beyond maintaining peace through the United Nations and encouraging free trade. Churchill was, however, more anxious than Roosevelt about Soviet aims in post-war Europe and the Mediterranean. For his part Stalin felt that the grand alliance of the war years and Soviet victories over Germany had enhanced the Soviet Union's status as a great power and entitled it to secure and consolidate a sphere of influence in Eastern Europe and elsewhere. Given the huge Soviet wartime sacrifices, Britain and the United States felt bound, during the wartime conferences in Teheran and Yalta, to acknowledge Moscow's hegemony in the countries 'liberated' by the Red Army. In the aftermath of the Second World War, the Soviet sphere of influence expanded from Central Europe, to Northern Europe and to the Far East, to include Manchuria, North Korea and Sakhalin.

During 1946 Britain, the United States, and the Soviet Union became conscious of the deterioration of the wartime grand alliance. They began to resist what they perceived to be Stalin's ambitions in Turkey, Iran and Greece. In Greece, a communist led guerrilla movement was attempting to overthrow the British-backed government in Athens. In February 1947 Britain informed the United States that it could no longer afford to sustain its present economic and military aid to Greece and Turkey, which also felt threatened by the Soviet Union. America responded to this by taking over Britain's responsibilities in Greece and Turkey and in the Truman Doctrine on 12 March 1947 the President, in order to secure Congressional funding, elevated the issue into a global struggle between freedom and political oppression. Then, in June 1947, the Marshall Plan was inaugurated which guaranteed Europe's economic recovery and strengthened the West's efforts to keep Communism at bay. With the failure of the London Conference of Foreign Ministers in December 1947, the United States, Britain and France began to consolidate Western Europe against the Soviet Union starting with the merger of the French, British and American occupation zones in West Germany, a precursor of the final division of Germany between East and West after 1948.

The Soviet Union regarded the Marshall Plan as an American instrument to dominate Western Europe and challenge the Soviet Union. Its reaction in 1948 deepened the East–West antagonism. The Soviet Union tightened its grip on the Eastern European countries, and in 1948 the Czechoslovakian coup resulted in the replacement of the last Eastern European coalition government by a communist regime. In March 1948, the Western zones of Germany were invited to join the European Recovery programme (or the Marshall Plan) which was, for Stalin, the final blow. The Soviet Union responded with the blockade of the Western occupied zones in Berlin. By 1948 the world was irrevocably divided between East and West. Moreover, this went beyond a clash of rival national interests. The leaders and publics of both sides felt they were pursuing broader, loftier goals. The Cold War was made more potent by being a conflict about both power and ideology.

After 1949, both sides concluded that the Cold War would be a lengthy and bitter struggle. The Soviet Union's successful explosion of an atomic device in 1949 resulted in a nuclear arms race between the two superpowers. The establishment of Mao's Communist China in 1949, and the outbreak of the Korean War in the following year meant that the Cold War had now spread to the other side of the Eurasian continent, with the West convinced that the Soviet Union was prepared to use surrogate troops – North Korean and Communist Chinese – to expand its sphere of influence. By the time of Stalin's death in 1953, the division of Europe had hardened, Eastern Europe had become thoroughly communised, modelled largely on the Soviet political and economic system. Meanwhile, the rearmament of the West was proceeding in earnest.

Conclusion

The period between 1953 and 1963 saw the consolidation of the bipolar order. Western Europe became militarily stronger when NATO (formed in 1949) was strengthened by an increased American commitment during the Korean War, and especially by the close integration of American nuclear weapons in NATO, and by the inclusion of Western Germany in the organisation in 1955, and economically after the formation of the Common Market in 1958. The Soviet Union's policies towards Eastern Europe were more haphazard: Stalin had already lost Yugoslavia in June 1948 when that country was expelled from the Cominform for actions taken independently of Moscow. However Tito's control of Yugoslavia was total and Stalin was unable to secure his overthrow. With the breaking of all economic and military links between Yugoslavia and the Eastern bloc, Tito was forced to seek financial and military assistance from the West. Then in February 1956 Khrushchev, at the 20th Party Congress, denounced Stalin's terror, and this, and the new Kremlin's slogan of peaceful coexistence with the West created difficulties for Soviet control of its satellites. There had already been an uprising in East Germany in 1953, and this was followed in 1956 by unrest in Poland and an uprising against Communist rule in Hungary in 1956. The Red Army crushed the Hungarian revolt, while tougher Soviet controls were thereafter imposed on the satellites. The Cold War was further globalised during this decade with the emergence of Soviet–Chinese–American rivalry for influence in the Third World – South East Asia, the Middle East, Africa, and Central and Latin America. China had been angered by Khrushchev's insistence on peaceful co-existence and, as a result, relations between the two countries had begun to deteriorate in the late 1950s culminating in the withdrawal of Soviet nuclear and other experts from China. The 1960s saw serious cross-border clashes. The accumulation of nuclear arsenals and advances in missile technology further poisoned American–Soviet relations. Fears of a nuclear war between the two superpowers were only slightly reduced by the Geneva Summit conference in 1955, and re-emerged in a more dramatic and dangerous form during the Cuban Missile Crisis in 1962.

However, after the Cuban missile crisis the bipolar system became less rigid. Nowhere was this more clearly demonstrated than in the rise of détente in Europe. After the withdrawal of

165

France from NATO's military command structure in 1966, West Germany negotiated a détente with Moscow, and the United States and Western Europe, including Britain, followed up this initiative during the first half of the 1970s by concluding a four-power agreement on Berlin and by signing the Helsinki Act in 1975. However, this regional détente was restricted to Europe, and even within Europe the key to the final resolution of the German question was still held by the Soviet Union.

America's involvement in the Third World also began to threaten the bipolar system. The lengthy and bloody war in Vietnam severely undermined the US economy and caused the United States to lose its credibility as the leader of the Western world. President Nixon's détente with Beijing and Moscow in 1971–1972 paved the way for America's disengagement from Vietnam. The two superpowers also entered into strategic arms negotiations, signing the SALT I treaty in 1972. Some scholars argue that détente brought real benefits: normalisation of relations with China lessened a source of hostility and put pressure on the Soviet Union. But détente did not survive. American conservatives claimed that it benefited the Soviet Union, which seemed confirmed by Moscow's efforts to expand its influence in the Third World, which led to another tense period of Cold War – the so-called 'new Cold War'.

The Soviet Union now felt more secure about its superpower status in Europe and in the nuclear sphere, and began to embark on an intensive effort to project its influence over the new revolutionary movements which were sweeping across Africa, the Middle East, and Central America. The Soviet Union and Cuban troops intervened in the Angolan civil war in 1975, in conflicts in Ethiopia and Somalia in 1977 and 1978, and, finally, in 1979, the Soviet Union invaded Afghanistan to sustain the faltering Communist leadership in Kabul. In November of the same year, Iranian radicals seized American diplomats in Teheran, and these hostages were not released until the Reagan administration came to power. By the mid-1970s, the Soviet Union had achieved strategic nuclear parity with the USA, and continued to modernise its nuclear arsenals, deploying the Backfire bomber and new intermediate-range nuclear forces, SS-20s.

By the time Reagan was elected President in 1981, the United States had been humiliated by the Iranian hostage crisis and was convinced that it was being outmanoeuvred by the Soviet Union in the Third World and in the nuclear arms race. The Reagan administration called for the restoration and revitalisation of a 'strong America' in the face of the Soviet threat, increased its armaments production and engaged in a more active policy towards the Third World. An anti-communist propaganda campaign was initiated when Reagan described the Soviet Union as an 'evil empire', the ratification of the SALT treaty was shelved, and new American missiles were deployed in Europe. This tough American stance angered the Soviet Union, whose representatives walked out of the superpower arms negotiations in the autumn of 1983. Once Reagan's rearmament programme, including Star Wars or SDI, was in place, and United States' self-confidence had been restored, the president was ready to open a dialogue with the Soviet Union, and after 1985, this led to the denouement of the Cold War.

The end of the Cold War was facilitated by the appointment of an active reformist leader in the Kremlin, Mikhail Gorbachev. Faced with major economic problems, he embarked on *perestroika* and *glasnost* as a means of integrating the Soviet Union into the Western capitalist world, to end the Soviet confrontational stance towards the West and to re-build the Soviet Union as a peaceful and pro-Western country. Although his domestic policies were ultimately unsuccessful, his foreign policy achieved agreement with the West for substantial reductions in the number of Soviet troops and nuclear weapons in Europe as well as agreements which ended Soviet–American interventions in the Third World. Gorbachev's term of office also witnessed the collapse of communist power in Eastern Europe. The majority of these countries managed the transition from communism peacefully – only Romania and Yugoslavia experienced violent internal conflict.

The Cold War's demise meant that Communism could no longer provide a unifying political force to hold the Eastern bloc together. This in turn released long suppressed nationalist feelings and pressures for freedom and independence in the former Soviet Republics, although these tendencies were often countered by the deep ethnical and religious divisions in many of these countries. While Czechoslovakia was peacefully broken up into two sovereign states through the 'Velvet divorce', the same did not apply to Yugoslavia. This federal state was made up of six republics – Serbia, Croatia, Bosnia-Herzegovina, Macedonia, Slovenia and Montenegro – and two autonomous regions – Vojvodina and Kosovo. After 1989, civil war broke out between the Serbs and Croats and then the conflict spread to Bosnia. The Serbian Communist leader, Slobodan Milosevic, was determined to assert Serbian hegemony by force over the other republics and in the Serbian elections in November 1989 he secured a majority for his Communist Party (later renamed the Serbian Socialist Party). By the end of 1991, Yugoslavia had practically ceased to exist, with the Yugoslavian federation consisting of only Serbia and Montenegro. The 1990s (the first decade after the Cold War) saw the spread of bloody inter-ethnic military conflict into Bosnia, Macedonia and Kosovo, which required military intervention by the UN and NATO.

Elsewhere in the former socialist eastern European states developments were more positive. East Germany was merged with the Federal Republic of Germany after the epoch-making fall of the Berlin Wall on 9–10 November 1989. Its reunification was agreed by the great powers in September 1990. The other former socialist countries found the end of communism as a political force a welcome relief after decades of authoritarian government. However their subsequent move towards a market based economy and democratisation led to many of them experiencing worsening social and economic conditions. The majority sought membership of NATO and the European Union (EU). NATO enlargement eastwards began with the inclusion of Hungary, Poland, and the Czech Republic in 1997. In 2004 Bulgaria, Estonia, Latvia, Lithuania, Romania, Slovakia and Slovenia joined NATO. The EU now includes all of these countries, except Bulgaria, plus Cyprus and Malta. Meanwhile, the Soviet Union collapsed on 25 December 1991 and was broken up into fifteen republics, while Gorbachev resigned as Soviet president.

Thus, the end of the Cold War allowed Europe to become 'whole and free' as President Bush proclaimed in the summer of 1990, and the Western order has prevailed as a result of the defeat of Communism. If the Cold War signified a 'long peace', charac-terised by the lack of military conflicts between the great powers, its end threatened a more unstable period of international relations. This certainly was true in the case of the outbreak of the civil war in Yugoslavia, though the rest of Europe has remained relatively peaceful. The urgent concerns in the post-Cold War world may not be about the resurgence of military conflict between the great powers, but about tackling problems within sovereign states, the consequences of a globalised economy and the emerging antagonism towards the West from elements in the non-Western world, which culminated in the September 11 attack on the USA. The triumphalism of some Americans about the Cold War victory of democracy and market economics might well have exacerbated these questions. How these issues will develop is unclear. If the forty-five years after 1945 were dominated by a geopolitical and ideological struggle between the two superpower blocs, the new era is likely to be more complicated, now that one ideology, communism, has all but disappeared and the United States is the only superpower.

Bibliography

[1] Dean Acheson, *Present at the Creation: My Years in the State Department* (New York, 1969). An elegantly written account by Truman's last Secretary of State, who was the chief architect of containment.

[2] G.M. Alexander, *The Prelude to the Truman Doctrine: British Policy in Greece 1944–1947* (Oxford, 1982). The Truman Doctrine was the first overt expression of American support for Western security. This book examines the background of Britain's intervention in the Greek civil war.

[3] Gar Alperovitz, *Atomic Diplomacy: Hiroshima and Potsdam* (New York, 1965). A 'New Left' historian who believes that the atomic bomb was intended as much to blackmail the Soviet Union into making concessions as to serve as an instrument to defeat Japan.

[4] Stephen E. Ambrose, *Rise to Globalism: American Foreign Policy since 1938* (Baltimore, various editions, 1970–). A useful textbook by one of the leading historians of the Cold War.

[5] Stephen E. Ambrose, *Eisenhower: The President 1952–1969*, Vol. II (London, 1984). An account of Eisenhower's internal and foreign policy based on his letters and papers, which is sympathetic to the President's achievements.

[6] Stephen E. Ambrose, *Nixon: The Education of a Politician, 1913–1962* (New York, 1982). This volume covers his earlier years as US Senator and Vice-President. It tries hard to be objective and to show that Nixon was not as black as he was painted by his contemporaries.

[7] Stephen E. Ambrose, *Nixon: The Triumph of a Politician, 1962–72* (New York, 1989). Ambrose captures his contradictory qualities: 'Nixon deserved to be re-elected and deserved to be repudiated'; and his darker side, for he 'was not planning how to bring people together ... but rather to destroy his enemies'.

[8] Terry H. Anderson, *The United States, Great Britain and the Cold War 1944–1947* (Missouri, 1981). A scholarly account of Anglo-American relations on the eve of the Cold War.

[9] Christopher Andrew and Oleg Gordievsky, *KGB* (London, 1990).

[10] D.R. Ashton, *In Search of Détente: The Politics of East–West Relations since 1945* (London, 1989).

[11]   Richard A. Asiano, *American Defense Policy from Eisenhower to Kennedy: The Politics of Changing Military Requirements* (Ohio, 1975). A comprehensive account of the vicissitudes of American defence policy from Sputnik to the presidential election of John F. Kennedy.

[12]   James A. Baker, *The Politics of Diplomacy* (New York, 1995). Gives a good sense of his temperament, views and working habits (he was wary of the State Department officials).

[13]   John Baylis, *Anglo-American Defence Relations 1939–1980: The Special Relationship* (London, 1982). A short but judicious assessment of the 'special relationship' in defence matters.

[14]   Antony Best, Jussi M. Hanhimäki, Joseph A. Maiolo, Kirsten E. Schulze, *International History of the Twentieth Century* (London, 2004). A clear, reliable account; less detailed than Young and Kent's study.

[15]   James Bill, *The Eagle and the Lion* (New Haven, 1988).

[16]   Charles E. Bohlen, *Witness to History 1929–1969* (New York, 1973). The memoirs of a senior American diplomat who played a leading role in many of the crises affecting the Soviet Union and the United States after 1945.

[17]   Willy Brandt, *People and Politics* (London, 1978). Provides valuable insights into Brandt's views and Germany's situation in the 1960s and 1970s.

[18]   Piers Brendon, *Ike: The Life and Times of Dwight D. Eisenhower* (London, 1987). A critical biography of Eisenhower.

[19]   Peter Boyle, *American–Soviet Relations* (London, 1993). A clear and thorough study.

[20]   Alan Bullock, *Ernest Bevin: Foreign Secretary 1945–1951* (London, 1983). This excellent biography is essential reading if the Labour government's foreign policy is to be correctly understood. Bevin successfully gambled on an American commitment to European defence.

[21]   George Bush and Brent Scowcroft, *A World Transformed* (New York, 1998). Valuable for the thinking behind policy but a curiously structured book: each chapter has separate contributions by each author.

[22]   Jimmy Carter, *Keeping Faith* (London, 1982).

[23]   Gordon Chang, *Friends and Enemies: The United States, China and the Soviet Union* (Stanford, California, 1989).

[24]   Richard Crockatt, *The Fifty Years War: The United States and the Soviet Union in World Politics, 1941–1991* (London, 1995).

[25]   Robert Dallek, *Franklin D. Roosevelt and American Foreign Policy 1932–1945* (New York, 1979). An outstanding favourable account of Roosevelt's foreign policy.

[26]   Robert Dallek, *John F. Kennedy: An Unfinished Life 1917–1963* (London, 2003). An impressive study that gives the fullest picture yet of JFK's poor health.

[27]   Robert Dallek, *Lone Star Rising: Lyndon Johnson and His Times, 1908–1960* (New York, 1991).

[28] Robert Dallek, *Flawed Giant: Lyndon and His Times, 1961–1973* (New York, 1998).

[29] Gerard J. DeGroot, *A Noble Cause? America and the Vietnam War* (London, 2000). An adept compact study.

[30] A.W. De Porte, *Europe between the Superpowers: The Enduring Balance* (London, 1979). A stimulating analysis of the European States system and its post-1945 role between the Soviet Union and the United States.

[31] Robert A. Divine, *Roosevelt and World War II* (New York, 1969). A rather critical discussion of Roosevelt's handling of foreign affairs.

[32] Robert A. Divine, *Blowing on the Wind: The Nuclear Test Ban Debate 1954–1960* (New York, 1981). A sophisticated analysis of the long and unsuccessful discussions on a test ban treaty in the 1950s in the face of the increasing danger from nuclear fall-out.

[33] Robert A. Divine, *Eisenhower and the Cold War* (Oxford, 1981). The development of the Cold War in the 1950s.

[34] Saki Dockrill, *Eisenhower's New Look National Security Policy, 1953–61* (Basingstoke, 1996) A revisionist monograph based on extensive research, it concludes that 'the president was an astute and imaginative statesman' who in the end failed to make the New Look acceptable to the Pentagon or to America's allies.

[35] *Documents on British Policy Overseas*, 3rd Series, Vols I–III (London, 2001) Very useful British documents on relations with the Soviet Union, *1968–1976*, many published ahead of their release in the archives.

[36] John Dumbrell, *The Carter Presidency: A Re-evaluation* 2nd edn (Manchester, 1995). A powerful case for Carter's merits.

[37] J.P.D. Dunbabin, *The Cold War. The Great Powers and their Allies* (London, 1994). Contains a great deal of valuable information and analysis.

[38] Fred Emery, *Watergate* (London, 1994). The companion to the BBC TV series which utilised extensive interviews with key individuals.

[39] Herbert Feis, *From Trust to Terror: The Onset of the Cold War, 1945–50* (New York, 1970).

[40] Herbert Feis, *Between War and Peace: The Potsdam Conference* (Princeton, 1960).

[41] Herbert Feis, *Churchill, Roosevelt, Stalin: The War they Waged and the Peace they Sought* (Princeton, 1957). Although overtaken in many respects by subsequent research, Feis's orthodox accounts of the first years of the Cold War contain useful information.

[42] Lawrence Freedman, *The Evolution of Nuclear Strategy* (London, 1982). Essential reading if the impact of nuclear weapons on strategic thinking and on superpower relations is to be fully understood.

[43] Lawrence Freedman, *Kennedy's Wars: Berlin, Laos, Cuba and Vietnam* (Oxford, 2001). Persuasive in its favourable interpretation of Kennedy.

[44] Edward Fursdon, *The European Defence Community: A History* (London, 1980). A sound account of the abortive attempt to reconcile West German rearmament with French fears of a renewal of the German threat.

[45] John Lewis Gaddis, *The United States and the Origins of the Cold War 1941–1947* (New York, 1972). A fascinating account of how American opinion about the Soviet Union changed so dramatically during and after the Second World War.

[46] John Lewis Gaddis, *Strategies of Containment: A Critical Appraisal of Post War American Security Policy* (Oxford, 1982). A subtle and astute analysis of American national security policy to 1976 grounded in archival research and taking as its base George Kennan's influence on the containment debate.

[47] John Lewis Gaddis, *The United States and the End of the Cold War* (Oxford, 1992).

[48] John Lewis Gaddis, *We Now Know: Rethinking the Cold War* (Oxford, 1997). An impressive survey.

[49] Raymond L. Garthoff, *Détente and Confrontation* 2nd edn (Washington, 1994). A magisterial account.

[50] Marc Jason Gilbert (ed.), *Why the North Won the Vietnam War* (New York, 2002) A valuable collection of essays on a variety of subjects relevant to the United States' defeat in Vietnam.

[51] Norman A. Graebner, *Cold War Diplomacy: American Foreign Policy 1945–1975* (London, 1977). This interpretation, by one of the leading moderate revisionist writers, suggests that the root cause of America's dilemma in handling the Cold War has been its historic tendency to universalise its ideals which, after 1947, caused it to assume global commitments which no nation, however strong, could for long sustain.

[52] Norman A. Graebner (ed.), *The National Security: Its Theory and Practice 1945–1960* (Oxford, 1986). A useful collection of essays by younger American historians on how the Truman and Eisenhower administrations dealt with the pressures and problems of the Cold War.

[53] John Robert Greene, *The Presidency of Gerald R. Ford* (Lawrence, Kansas, 1995)

[54] Albert Grosser, *The Western Alliance: European–American Relations since* 1945 (London, 1980). A discussion of European perceptions of their relationship with the United States after the Second World War.

[55] Louis Hallé, *The Cold War as History* (New York, 1967). A revisionist critique of the origins of the Cold War, suggesting that the United States over-reacted to what were often defensive Soviet moves after 1945.

[56] Jussi Hanhimäki and Odd Arne Westad (eds), *The Cold War: A History in Documents* (Oxford, 2003). A useful selection of documents on a range of themes, including high politics, culture and espionage, with succinct commentaries on the topics.

[57] Wolfram F. Hanrieder, *Germany, America and Europe. Forty Years of German Foreign Policy* (New Haven, Connecticut, 1989)

[58] Fraser J. Harbutt, *The Iron Curtain: Churchill, America and the Origins of the Cold War* (London, 1987). A detailed, but not entirely convincing, analysis of Churchill's role in converting American public opinion from a detached pro-Soviet view of international affairs to one of full-blown support for Britain and its overseas interests.

[59] Max Hastings, *The Korean War* (London, 1987). The military aspects of the Korean War.

[60] Gregg Herken, *The Winning Weapon: The Atomic Bomb in the Cold War 1945–50* (New York, 1982).

[61] Townsend Hoopes, *The Devil and John Foster Dulles* (Boston, 1973). A hard hitting critique of the foreign policy of Dulles.

[62] Timothy P. Ireland, *Creating the Entangling Alliance: The Origins of NATO* (London, 1981). The United States hoped that its contribution to NATO would be psychological encouragement to the Europeans and that its military assistance would enable them to stand on their own feet and not depend too much on American troops.

[63] Burton I. Kaufman, *The Presidency of James Earl Carter, Jr* (Lawrence, Kansas, 1993). More critical than Dumbrell's study.

[64] George F. Kennan, *Memoirs 1925–1950* (Boston, 1967) and *Memoirs 1950–1963* (Boston, 1972). Kennan's role in United States diplomacy during the turbulent years after 1945 when relations with the Soviet Union reached their lowest ebb.

[65] Robert F. Kennedy, *Thirteen Years: A Memoir of the Cuban Missile Crisis* (New York, 1965). A personal account of how the crisis was handled by President Kennedy's brother, who was Attorney General.

[66] Douglas Kinnard, *President Eisenhower and Strategy Management: A Study in Defense Politics* (Lexington, 1977).

[67] Henry A. Kissinger, *Nuclear Weapons and Foreign Policy* (New York, 1957). A contribution to the critique of Eisenhower's 'Massive Retaliation' Doctrine by the historian who subsequently became President Nixon's Secretary of State.

[68] Henry Kissinger, *White House Years* (Boston, 1979).

[69] Henry Kissinger, *Years of Upheaval* (Boston, 1982).

[70] Henry Kissinger, *Years of Renewal* (New York, 1998). Each volume provides massive details and incisive portraits of key individuals. Nevertheless, the books are skilful cases for the importance of Kissinger's role.

[71] Joyce and Gabriel Kolko, *The Limits of Power: The World and United States Foreign Policy 1945–1954* (New York, 1972). A 'New Left' interpretation of the Cold War which blames American economic imperialism for the post-1945 events.

[72] Igor Korchilov, *Translating History* (London, 1997). A useful insight into Soviet thinking from Gorbachev's translator.

[73] B.R. Kuniholm, *The Origins of the Cold War in the Near East: Great Power Conflict in Iran, Turkey and Greece* (Princeton, 1980). Case studies of specific areas in the Near East, in which the Cold War originated, based on research in American archives.

[74] Walter, LaFeber, *America, Russia and the Cold War 1945–1980* (New York, 1980). A sound standard textbook.

[75] Carl A. Linden, *Khrushchev and the Soviet Leadership 1957–1964* (Maryland, 1966). An interesting account of Khrushchev's internal and external struggles from Sputnik to his fall from power.

[76] Callum MacDonald, *Korea: The War before Vietnam* (London, 1986). A balanced interpretation of the political and diplomatic background to the Korean War.

[77] Michael Mandelbaum, *The Nuclear Revolution: International Politics Before and After Hiroshima* (New York, 1981).

[78] Michael Mandelbaum, *The Nuclear Question: The United States and Nuclear Weapons* (New York, 1979). The impact of the atomic bomb on international relations and on American foreign policy during the Cold War.

[79] Vojtech Mastny, *Russia's Road to the Cold War: Diplomacy, Warfare and the Politics of Communism 1941–45* (New York, 1979). Stalin's search for absolute security both inside and outside the Soviet Union inevitably resulted, the author claims, in a clash with the West after the Second World War.

[80] William McCagg, *Stalin Embattled: 1943–1948* (Detroit, 1978). Stalin was by no means all-powerful and secure towards the end of the Second World War, as contemporaries believed, and this book deals with his struggle to re-establish his absolute authority after 1943.

[81] Robert McMahon, *The Cold War* (Oxford, 2003). An excellent short study that includes a section on the domestic impact of the Cold War.

[82] David Mervin, *Ronald Reagan and the American Presidency* (London, 1990).

[83] David Mervin, *George Bush and the Guardianship Presidency* (Basingstoke, 1998). Like its predecessor on Reagan, this is a succinct and effective early study.

[84] Richard Nixon, *RN: The Memoirs of Richard Nixon* (London, 1978).

[85] Joseph L. Nogee and Robert H. Donaldson, *Soviet Foreign Policy since World War II* (Oxford, 1984). A general survey of Soviet foreign policy down to the 1980s.

[86] Yonusuke Nagai and Akira Iriye (eds), *The Origins of the Cold War in Asia* (New York, 1977). A useful collection of essays on the Asian dimension of the Cold War.

[87] Don Oberdorfer, *From the Cold War to a New Era* (Baltimore, 1998). An impressive, vivid study by a journalist who reported events and has interviewed an extensive range of politicians and officials in both Russia and the United States. He focuses mainly on the central figures and their negotiations.

[88]   Robert Osgood, *Limited War: The Challenge to American Strategy* (New York, 1957). One of the more perceptive critics of Eisenhower's 'Massive Retaliation' Doctrine.

[89]   Chester J. Pach and Elmo Richardson, *The Presidency of Dwight D. Eisenhower* (Lawrence, Kansas, 1991). An interesting survey of domestic, defence and foreign policies which, while revisionist in its treatment of Eisenhower as a skilful leader, does not accept that the president's policies were as successful as many revisionists claim.

[90]   Herbert S. Parmet, *JFK: The Presidency of John F. Kennedy* (London, 1984). A sound biography but less impressive than Dallek or Freedman.

[91]   Thomas G. Paterson, *Postwar Reconstruction and the Origins of the Cold War* (London, 1973). The economic aspects of the Soviet–American confrontation after 1945.

[92]   Thomas G. Paterson, J. Garry Clifford and Kenneth J. Hagan, *American Foreign Relations. A History Since 1895* 4th edn (Lexington, Massachusetts, 1995).

[93]   William Quandt, *Camp David* (Washington, 1986).

[94]   Ronald Reagan, *An American Life* (London, 1990). Like the man, pleasant, easy going and not very penetrating, but it contains some useful material.

[95]   David Reynolds (ed.), *The Origins of the Cold War in Europe: International Perspectives* (New Haven, Connecticut, 1994).

[96]   David Reynolds, *One World Divisible: A Global History Since 1945* (London, 2000). Like all his work, this is a commendably thorough and perceptive volume.

[97]   Victor Rothwell, *Britain and the Cold War 1941–1947* (London, 1982). This should really have been entitled 'The British Foreign Office and the Cold War' but it is none the worse for that.

[98]   Kevin Ruane, *War and Revolution in Vietnam 1930–75* (London, 1998). A clear and concise analysis based on a wide selection of secondary sources.

[99]   Mike Sewell, *The Cold War* (Cambridge, 2002).

[100] George P. Shultz, *Triumph and Turmoil* (New York, 1993). A detailed volume that offers insights from a crucial figure.

[101] Robert D. Schulzinger, *Henry Kissinger: Doctor of Diplomacy* (New York, 1989).

[102] Robert D. Schulzinger, *American Diplomacy in the Twentieth Century* 3rd edn (New York, 1994).

[103] Robert D. Schulzinger, *A Time of War* (New York, 1997).

[104] John Spanier, *American Foreign Policy since World War II* (New York, various editions, 1965–).

[105] William Stueck, *The Korean War: An International History* (Princeton, 1995). An excellent study that utilises a wide range of sources.

[106] Strobe Talbott, *Endgame: The Inside Story of SALT II* (New York, 1979).

[107] Strobe Talbott (trans. and ed.), *Khrushchev Remembers* (Boston, 1970). Initially suspected of being a forgery, these memoirs are now generally accepted by historians as being authentic, although the testimony is one-sided and unreliable.

[108] William Taubman, *Stalin's American Policy: from Entente to Détente to Cold War* (New York, 1982).

[109] Adam B. Ulam, *The Rivals: America and Russia since World War II* (New York, 1975).

[110] Martin Walker, *The Cold War* (London, 1994). Gives more attention to economics than most studies.

[111] Donald Cameron Watt, *Succeeding John Bull: America in Britain's Place 1900–1975* (Cambridge, 1984). A thought-provoking analysis of the causes and consequences of Britain's displacement by the United States as a world power.

[112] Odd Arne Westad (ed.), *The Fall of Détente: Soviet–American Relations during the Carter Years* (Oslo, 1997).

[113] Russell F. Weigley, *The American Way of War: History of United States Strategy and Military Policy* (New York, 1973). Part V of this history deals with the frustrations experienced by the American military in a post-war world where they have had to accept considerably less than total victory over an opponent.

[114] Kieran Williams, *The Prague Spring and Its Aftermath* (Cambridge, 1997).

[115] William Appleman Williams, *The Tragedy of American Diplomacy* (New York, 1959). An elegantly written 'New Left' critique of American Cold War policy after 1945.

[116] Gary Wills, *Reagan's America* (London, 1988).

[117] Randall Bennett Woods and Howard Jones, *Dawning of the Cold War* (Athens, Georgia, 1991). A thorough and judicious study of 1945–1950.

[118] Daniel Yergin, *Shattered Peace: The Origins of the Cold War and the National Security State* (Boston, 1977). The US defence establishment's perceptions of the Soviet danger down to 1950, based on archival research in the USA.

[119] John W. Young, *The Longman Companion to Cold War and Detente, 1941–1991* (London, 1993).

[120] John W. Young and John Kent, *International Relations Since 1945: A Global History* (Oxford, 2004). A comprehensive, accessible survey.

[121] Philip Zelikow and Condoleeza Rice, *Germany Unified and Europe Transformed* (Cambridge, Massachusetts, 1995). An impressive early study by two officials: a career diplomat turned academic and an academic who became Secretary of State in 2005.

[122] Vladislav Zubok and Constantine Pleshakov, *Inside the Kremlin's Cold War: From Stalin to Khrushchev* (Cambridge, Massachusetts, 1996). A broad analysis based on recently opened Soviet archives and interviews with Soviet survivors of the early Cold War period, it draws attention to Stalin's diplomatic blunders after 1945.

Websites

www.cnn.com/SPECIALS/coldwar   CNN site for its excellent twenty-four part documentary series Cold War.

www.coldwar.org   Cold War Museum website.

wwwics.si.edu   Cold War International History Project, Washington. It issues a Bulletin containing translated documents and articles on them. It also releases working papers on Cold War themes.

www.state.gov/r/pa/ho/frus   *Foreign Relations of the United States*, whose printed volumes begin in 1861, provides the official documentary record of US foreign policy. There are online versions available for 1961 onwards.

www.isn.ethz.ch/php   Parallel history project which examines NATO and the Warsaw Pact in parallel.

www.gwu.edu/nsa   National Security Archive which is assiduous in locating and publishing new materials.

Index

Index

Britain, 4, 10–14, 15–18, 20–1, 26,
29, 37–8, 40–1, 43, 46, 48–50, 52,
59, 61, 64–7, 70–2, 76, 82–3, 87,
89–90, 105, 121, 127–8, 148,
156–7, 163–4, 166
Brosio, Manlio, 121
Brown, Harold, 123–4, 128, 130
Brussels Pact, 43–4, 70
Brzezinski, Zbigniew, 100, 123–6,
128–30
Bulganin, Marshal, 63, 73
Bulgaria, 16, 26, 30, 37, 47, 92,
155, 168
Burma, 65
Bush, George, 5, 146–7, 152–3,
156–8, 168
Byrnes, James F., 28–31, 35–7, 53

Caetano, 119
California, 135
Cambodia, 80, 107–8, 119, 130,
137, 150–1
Canada, 34, 44, 46
Carlucci, Frank, 136, 141
Carter Doctrine, 134
Carter, Jimmy, 100, 121,
123–37, 142
Castro, Fidel, 75, 78, 83
Caucasian republic, 159
Ceausescu, Nicolae, 93, 155
Central African Federation, 82
Central Europe, 33, 39, 47, 53–4,
68, 71, 121, 152, 154, 156, 163
Central Intelligence Agency (CIA),
62–3, 75, 78, 80, 82, 117, 123,
137, 152, 156
Central Treaty Organisation,
(Baghdad Pact), 65, 67
Charter of Paris (1989), 158
Cheney, Dick, 153
Chernenko, Konstantin, 140,
142–3, 146–7
Chernobyl, 145
Chiang Kai-shek, 21, 45, 47, 50,
54–5, 59, 69
Chile, 113–15, 119, 123
Chilean Christian Democrat
Party, 114

Chilean National Congress, 114
Chilean Nationalist Party, 114
China, 6, 9, 15–16, 18, 21, 45–50,
54–5, 58, 61, 63–5, 68–9,
72–4, 83, 86, 88, 91, 93, 96–8,
103, 107–11, 122, 124,
128–30, 151–2, 154, 164–6
China lobby, 45–6, 50, 55
Churchill, Winston S., 11–14,
16–19, 22, 25, 27, 31, 33–6,
53, 163
'Civic Forum', 155
Clay, General Lucius D., 42
Clifford, Clark, 99
Columbia University, 124
Cominform (Communist
Information Bureau), 40, 165
Comintern (Communist
International), 17
Committee of State Security (KGB),
29, 139–40, 144, 159–60
Committee on the Present
Danger, 132
Commonwealth of Independent
States, (CIS), 160
Conference on Security and
Cooperation in Europe,
1972–3, (CSCE), 104, 106,
120, 121
Congo, (Belgian until 1960), The,
28, 36, 81–3
Contras, 137, 141
Conventional Forces in Europe
Treaty (CFE), 158
Cox, Archibald, 117
Croatia, 168
Cronkite, Walter, 126
Cruise missiles, 128, 132, 137–40,
151
Cuba, 75, 78, 83–7, 101, 114, 119,
127–9, 137, 150, 166
Cuban missile crisis, 6, 83–9, 91,
101, 116, 165
Cyprus, 168
Czech Republic, 168
Czechoslovakia, 20, 22, 39–40, 54,
63, 65–6, 93, 101, 120, 154–5,
164, 168

180

Index